Rhythmical Alchemy Playshop

Volume #1 | Drum Circle Games

for Music Educators, School Teachers,
Recreational Drummers & Drum Circle Facilitators

by Arthur Hull
Edited by Angela Marie

Village Music Circles
Santa Cruz, CA

D1608627

Cover: photograph by Donna Welch Photography

Rhythmical Alchemy Playshop Volume #1, Drum Circle Games
Copyright © 2013 by Arthur Hull

Village Music Circles
108 Coalinga Way,
Santa Cruz, CA 95060
USA

Phone: (831) 458-1946
Fax: (831) 459-7215

www.drumcircle.com
outreach@drumcircle.com

Printed in China

Library of Congress Cataloging-in-Publication Data

Hull, Arthur 1947-
    Rhythmical Alchemy Playshop Volume #1, Drum Circle Games/Arthur Hull.
    Includes biographical references and index.
    ISBN #: 978-0-9724307-3-9
    1. Group rhythmic event facilitation–Instruction and study.   2. Community music–Instruction and study.
    3. Percussion instruments–Instruction and study.   4. Musical meter and rhythm–Instruction and study.

Rick Walker

Aryn Forrest Hull
at three years old,
performs for 50,000
in San Francisco.

Dedication

I dedicate this book to the childlike spontaneous rhythmical spirit
that lives inside all of us. Set it free. Let it play.

Table of Contents

Janet Planet

The Lincoln Park Performing Arts Charter School kids, and assistant facilitators whom I had the privilege of playing with for over a week during the DVD shoot.

Pictured: Top row to bottom row, from left to right

Row 1: Terry Edmondson, Sarah Landa, Marissa Kolarosky, Emily Pasquarelli, Kiersten Grey, Honor Sittig, Rick Parsons, Antonio Monteiro

Row 2: Michael Harb, Alyssa Janney, Sal Aloe, Joshua Worthing

Row 3: Ed Boas, Lauren Lang, Taylor Modro, Desiree Brown, Abbey Prepelka, Alana Young, Trey Singletary, Alex Castille, Janet Planet, Laurie "LaLa" Precht

Row 4: Lori Fithian, Emmilia Zimmel, Julianna Sacco, Kayla McQuillen, J.P. Coletta, Kyle Schwartz, Greg Whitt

Arthur Hull laying in front

Foreword:
Share Your Spirit
by Jim Oshinsky

Arthur Hull and I have long shared a dream of sorts:

- That the spirit of our circles would someday extend to every household and neighborhood and influence everyday musical experiences
- That our culture would allow everyone to be a drummer, a singer, and a musician, and not reserve such titles only for some elite and separate group
- That the music inside every individual would be encouraged and expressed rather than critiqued out of existence
- That the barriers between performer and audience would be more fluid and interactive, so that it would be common to be an active participant rather than a passive witness of musical arts.

Some dreams are worth our lifetimes.

Arthur and I have been brainstorming and sharing ideas for over 20 years. When we began, we were each near the start of our musical evangelical enterprises, spreading our passion for improvised community music. Arthur's lineage was from traditional percussion and from large group tribal experiences – "urban thunder drumming" amongst devout musical anarchists. I came from the musical equivalent of a small town – rock and folk ensembles, with a smattering of chamber music thrown in. Arthur was outgoing and comfortable in large groups. I was much more shy, at home in a quartet or a classroom. He was west coast California, I was east coast Noo Yawk. Prior to meeting Arthur, I would never have considered myself a drummer; my musical credentials have been earned on guitar and bass. But all of us, strings and skins alike, speak rhythm.

When Arthur and I first met there was not much in the way of training for prospective workshop leaders in the area of music improvisation. I had been collaborating with cellist David Darling in his organization, Music for People. Together with very mindful and compassionate colleagues, Music for People designed a training for music improvisation group leaders that presented melody, rhythm and harmony both as musical elements and as metaphors for interpersonal interactions. In this system, advanced trainees mentored beginning trainees, and the content of feedback was truthful, positive and supportive. This was part of the model I shared with Arthur Hull as we were sitting on the lakefront float at Omega Institute in Rhinebeck, NY.

When Arthur wrote Drum Circle Spirit, I was hoping it would contain some useful information for leading large groups that we could put to use in Music for People training. His book did more than that. Drum Circle Spirit set the standard for human potential and creativity leadership writing. He showed us what he had been learning; he put his knowledge base into clear and insightful language; he invented terms where none previously existed for the group phenomena he was discussing, and he modeled detailed self-examination by highlighting what he learned from his slip-ups along the way. Arthur gave us a collection of gems.

In his books and videos that have followed on the subject of Drum Circle Facilitation, Arthur has continued to share the knowledge that he and his drum circle colleagues worldwide have been gathering through their experiences and adventures. In each book he has broken down the process and the activities to more and more basic levels. The tone and clarity of his writing inspires drummers and facilitators to spread this important work and empower individuals while making highly connected music. Imagine hundreds of little Arthurs (without the hats, perhaps) reaching into the mainstream of music education and seeping into the music of our culture!

Arthur's guiding metaphor has long been "rhythmical alchemy," turning our musical experiences into deeper personal transformations. He sifts his teaching more finely with each pass through the concepts, and in his current series of books on Drum Circle Facilitation he makes the key learning experiences into games that are disarmingly simple, subtly nested within a humanistic mindset. His kind of Alchemy continues to transform people. This volume of Rhythmical Alchemy Playshop Drum Circle Games is Arthur's latest contribution to our shared dream of making rhythmical play ever more accessible to everyone. In his letters to drummers, guitarists, and colleagues, Arthur often signs off with the gentle urging, "Share Your Spirit." Exactly. Let's.

Arthur facilitates a rhythm game in Japan.

You multiply your daring a hundred-fold by sharing its fruits. You give your life away and, behold! a richer life comes back to you. This principle works through all of life: Our most valuable possessions are those which can be shared without lessening: those which, when shared, multiply. Our least valuable possessions are those which, when divided, are diminished.

— William H. Danforth, I Dare You

Acknowledgments

I have been facilitating Rhythmical Alchemy Playshops longer than I have been teaching people how to facilitate drum circles.

I started developing interactive rhythm games in schools, corporate team-building programs etc. to meet the needs of any particular constituency, educational, corporate, community or spiritual.

But the main part of the development of the Rhythmical Alchemy Playshop games and curriculum was due to my creating and using Rhythmical Alchemy Playshop, RAP, games in the personal growth movement programs at venues like Omega Institute in New York state, Esalen Institute on the Big Sur coast in California and at numerous Yoga Journal, Noetic Science, and Omega national conferences. Later I also facilitated RAPs regularly at the Infinity Foundation in Chicago as well as the Naropa Institute and Shambhala Mountain Center in Colorado.

The organizers of these personal growth institutions and conference events have changed hands many times during my formative development of the RAP games, but the consciousness of the people who attended these programs has continually challenged me to share with them the best of myself, my passion for rhythmical connection and spirit.

In particular I would like to acknowledge the support, mentoring and encouragement of the following people who believed in me when I was formulating what Rhythmical Alchemy is and can be.

- Greg Zolanka from the Omega Institute
- David Price of the Esalen Institute
- Nancy Grace Marder of the Infinity Foundation

- Charlotte Rotterdam, Naropa program coordinator, now with Shambhala
- Doug Wilson from the ROWE Retreat Center
- M.A. Bjarkman of the "Conference Works" who brought me into many Society for Humanistic Psychology and Noetic Science conferences

I would like to acknowledge and thank my good friend, rhythm teacher and life mentor Babatunde Olatunji (April 7, 1927 – April 6, 2003). Throughout our relationship, Babatunde continually encouraged me to find ways to make the exploration and expression of rhythmical spirit "accessible to those who have no interest in culturally-specific drumming."

In my early "Playshop" days at the Omega Institute, I met Jim Oshinsky. Jim was and still is, extensively involved in the Music for People organization founded by David Darling. When he shared a brief version of Music for People's workshop curriculum, it became obvious to both of us that we are walking parallel paths.

That meeting was the beginning of a more than 20-year relationship that has provided benefits to both of us. With Jim's advocacy, my first book, "Drum Circle Spirit," was incorporated into Music for People's curriculum.

I would like to thank Jim for his mentoring and friendship and for introducing me to an organization that walks the path of rhythmical and musical empowerment for all people.

I would also like to acknowledge and thank Remo D. Belli and his company REMO for their continuous support over the years for me and my mission of rhythmical evangelism.

This Book

This book series was created from the extensive notes that I took over the years while facilitating Rhythmical Alchemy Playshops.

With more than two weeks worth of games (sixty plus hours) that I had available in my RAP bag, one reason I created the notes was to help me remember what we did at a particular Playshop so that when I returned the next year, I could design a completely different event for the returnee participants.

Another reason for taking those notes was because at almost every RAP Playshop that I facilitated, a new game or game variation was discovered by me or the participants.

To the people who have attended the hundreds of Rhythmical Alchemy Playshops over the past 30 years, I am eternally grateful to you for sharing your spirit and your inspiration with me.

While participating in one of my "Layering In a Rhythm" games at a six-day RAP, Jim Oshinsky shared a Music for People ensemble game and adapted it to meet our percussion circle environment. It was the perfect next step in the "Layering" series.

With Jim's permission, and my thank you, I have incorporated it into our RAP community and share it with you in this book. The game is entitled "Layering In an Ensemble."

Also I would like to acknowledge and thank Mike DeMenno of the REMO Recreational Music Center for creating and adding his "Share Your Groove on the Run" game. I include it here in the "Share Your Groove" series. These games are wonderful gifts to our recreational drumming community.

Thank you to DRUM Magazine for their permission to include many of my RAP games that were published regularly in my Drum Circle Games column in their magazine, www.drummagazine.com.

Not a word from any of my books gets to print without the scrutiny of Angela Marie's amazing editing skills. In the almost 20 years of sitting next to Angela while she edits my work, her influence and mentoring has slowly turned me into a writer, whether I liked it or not. One of the reasons for sitting with Angela during the editing process is that she asks me the hard questions: What do you mean by this?, is this necessary to the point you're making?, or how can you say more with less? Her writing spirit now sits on my shoulder whispering to me every time I put pen to paper. My first draft of any book is always in ink.

I thank Larry Israel for some reorganization and final copy editing.

I would like to acknowledge Staci Sambol of Slub Design for her cover design, and for her great layout and formatting of yet another of my books.

Donna Welsh is a professional photographer on the island of Oahu, Hawaii. She is one of the few people I know who can consistently catch spirit with a camera. Donna has attended many of the community drum circles at the close of our annual Hawaii Facilitator's Playshop Trainings on the north shore of Oahu and played with her camera as much as her drum. I thank her for photographic contributions to this book, including the cover photo. Nearly all of the other photographs in this book were taken by the Village Music Circles staff or myself over the years.

As a young man in the early '90s, Peter Cerny would give me hand-painted dot drawings on tee shirts in exchange for taking my hand drum classes. As a fellow dot artist I appreciated his vision. Now a well-established artist in the San Francisco bay area, Peter's artwork has captured the spirit of much of Village Music Circle's message for many years. I thank him for the spirit of my words in visual form, and for the opportunity to use my own dot artwork in this book series.

Music Education Standards

Nellie Hill is one of our Village Music Circles Mentor graduates. As a VMC certified facilitator, REMO Health Rhythms facilitator, and certified life coach she now teaches workshops on music education related to drum circles and world music. One of her specialties is applying drum circle activities to the National Standards for Music Education and arts integration.

For many years Nellie has been my mentor in the area of music education in relationship to recreational drumming and interactive music games. She went through this book with a fine-tooth comb, and applied the National Standards for Music Education concepts to my drum circle games. I thank her for contributing that important piece to this book.

The DVD

The DVD included with this book is a result of a fantastic program. A big thank you goes to Alyssa Janney, manager of REMO Health Rhythms for connecting me to the Lincoln Park Performing Arts Charter School in Midland, Pennsylvania. She supported and encouraged me to do a RAP project with the kids in the drum circle study group at the school. Alyssa attended the program, and supported us through the process. Thank you also to REMO for gifting two sets of the REMO Arthurian Facilitator Sound Shapes, a Bahia Bass, and lots of drums and percussion.

Dr Berry Bittman and Christine Stevens presented REMO HealthRHYTHM events at the Performing Arts Center, inspiring the center to start regular drum circle classes at the school. Thank you for the inspiration. Thank you to Sal Aloe, Director of Partnerships and Special Projects at the Lincoln Park Performing Arts Center, for his work in helping to set up the program with the kids and film the Facilitator Training and the RAP games.

I would like to acknowledge Michael Harb and his film crew. Coordinating a four-camera shoot is not easy. By the end of the project, Mike took a couple of turns facilitating the group, using lessons he learned while behind the camera — not bad either!

I offer thanks to Rick Parsons and Antonio Montiero, the school's drum circle teachers, for their service to the kids. They did a great job with the high school kids who were at the shoot, and yes, because of their work with the kids, as Laurie "LaLa" Precht said, "It was like sitting down in a drum circle that was all shills."

A big heart felt thanks goes out to the Village Music Circle Facilitation Playshop Graduates who came to Pennsylvania from all over the country to be my helper facilitators for the project:

- Janet Planet from Los Angeles, California
- Greg Whitt from Raleigh, North Carolina
- Laurie (LaLa) Precht from Baltimore, Maryland
- Ed Boas from Cleveland, Ohio
- Alyssa Janney from Los Angeles, California
- Lori Fithian from Ann Arbor, Michigan
- Deke Kincaid from Pittsburgh, Pennsylvania

These people went out of their way to support both the program and me. I thank them for the sacrifices they had to make in their lives to travel from many places in the US to be at this project in Midland, Pennsylvania. I especially thank them all for sharing their Spirits with the kids.

...and Oh My God! THE KIDS!

My heart felt thank you goes out to the fantastic group of 40 young people from the Lincoln Park Performing Arts Charter School who committed themselves to this project. They used my two drum circle facilitation books as part of their curriculum so they knew the Arthurian verbal language, and had down the facilitation body language. They ignored the cameras during the shoot, but most importantly they were fearless, creative and spirited. Not only did they have 'A-Lot-O-Fun,' they made it fun for everyone involved. My two 'distractors' in the group ended up as my best facilitators. I have done facilitation courses with high school students before, but never had I had such a motivated, attentive group of young adults give back to me as much as I gave to them.

We had a snow day during that program where the school day was canceled due to a large snowstorm. That gave me an excuse to fly back to the Performing Arts Center a few weeks later to complete the Playshop program.

Between my first and second visits to Midland, Pennsylvania the kids in the drum circle study group at the Performing Arts Center took the REMO drum circle kit around to various schools in their district and took turns facilitating drum circle events. They continue to facilitate events today.

Ray Shaffer and I edited the video of the students' games to create the DVD that accompanies this book. I am very thankful for Ray's visual acuity and great editing techniques, as well as his ability to capture the spirit of the event that goes beyond the visual reference.

A big thank you to Janet Planet from LA, our Village Music Circles international Program Producer and Creative Director. Janet was our Producer/Director for the shoot. She took care of all the details, wrangled me, coordinated the camera crew, the high school kids, and our guest facilitators all at the same time. She even got into the circle and facilitated from time to time.

All the people mentioned above who were involved with the physical development of this book have an interlocking relationship with each other that goes back over many years. By coming together to work on a Village Music Circles book from time to time and sharing our unique talents with each other, we reaffirm our interconnectedness and our community.

I thank them all for sharing their talents and spirit in bringing this book series to fruition.

Arthur Hull

Introduction

This is the first volume of the Rhythmical Alchemy Playshop series. It focuses on hand drumming games for a group of players sitting in a circle facing each other. The drum circle games in this volume are designed for all the people in the circle to play some sort of drum. Many of these same games can be easily adapted to use all hand percussion or a mixture of both drums and percussion, and we still call the group a drum circle.

While these rhythm games offer fun and enjoyment for those who participate, they also teach the individuals about aspects of cooperative and collaborative rhythmical music making. Through the interactive process, participants receive information about actions that make a drum circle work, and about the specific elements that exist in the rhythms and music that they are creating. I call this experiential learning. All ages and levels of rhythmical experience can participate and learn at the same time, while having a lot of fun. Learning happens while players are having so much fun that they are not noticing that they are learning.

These rhythmical empowerment games are an open doorway into music education for people who have just begun their journey of rhythmical exploration, or who have been taught, or believe, that they are rhythmically or musically challenged.

These RAP games also serve veteran recreational drummers by showing them new and exciting ways to play with their friends. Drummers who have been on the path of learning culturally specific rhythms will benefit as they experience universal principles that permeate all drumming and rhythmaculture traditions. These games invite the culturally specific drummer to discover the power of their own rhythmical spirit and encourage them to explore and improvise beyond the limitations that the rhythms they have been learning may have unconsciously imposed upon them.

Drum Circle Games are good for a group coming together for the first time as well as for those recreational drummers who are meeting and drumming with each other on a regular basis. These games offer opportunities for agreement among drummers about elements needed to create a successful group rhythm. RAP games are formats for collaboration and agreement among a circle of players that enhance the experience for everyone involved.

Thinking of the elements offered in RAP as games rather than exercises empowers the group to create opportunities to learn group self-facilitation in a supportive and non-competitive environment. These drum circle games are designed to teach the players, through their own experiences, particular aspects of how to play in a collaborative drum circle ensemble.

Drum Circle Games offer fun experiential learning situations that depend on the players coming to consensus about agreements that govern their rhythmical and musical interaction. Once these agreements are made, the magic can begin.

Using the DVD

The accompanying DVD shows each of the RAP games being played by the high school kids of the Lincoln Park Performing Arts Charter School. This DVD provides a visual reference of how to use and facilitate these rhythm activities.

If you are looking for a specific type of game, such as an agreement game, a facilitated game or an orchestrated game (see "Types of Games" on page 29), you will easily find them listed on the DVD under the "Types of Games" menu.

Under the DVD chapter entitled "Games," you will find all of the games in the same order as they are listed in this book.

Why RAP?

As a rhythmical evangelist, my life is dedicated to creating an open doorway to the magic of self expression through rhythm. Something special happens when people gather and create a fun, interactive rhythmical experience together. Participating is easier than most people think possible. Playing together creates intimate interpersonal connections that transcend politics, gender, religion and age differences.

Drums and percussion are the most accessible instruments available. Making in-the-moment music together while playing these instruments places participants in a be-here-now state of consciousness. Being here now while exploring our rhythmical and musical spirits opens up ways to communicate beyond words in a safe, fun, collaborative and creative environment.

A Village Music Circles Rhythmical Alchemy Playshop™, or RAP, uses a series of interactive rhythm-based games to help people uncover, discover and recover their natural rhythmical spirit that they playfully possessed as children. I offer this series of games as an expression of my musical spirit to yours.

Our Rhythmical Alchemy Playshop has been designed to accommodate and showcase all levels of musical and rhythmical expertise at the same time. It makes no difference whether you are the mayor or the janitor, 10 years old or 100, rich or poor, have a lot of drumming and musical experience or none. A RAP-based event provides a safe, supportive container for rhythmical alchemy, and offers equal chances for participation and creativity for all participants.

The RAP games offered in this series of books make it possible to create a safe environment for personal rhythm exploration, expression and learning. They provide formats for collaboration and agreement among a circle of players. The games are sets of agreements which everyone adheres to in order to create a fun and exciting rhythmical experience together.

Most games of sport have agreements concerning the rules that govern the competition, and there are winners and losers. Recreational drum circle games also have agreements. These agreements govern participants' interactive rhythmical cooperation and challenges so that they all win as they accomplish their mutual goal of making music together.

Drum circle games offer each person a chance to shine and speak their spirit through their instrument. By playing these games they learn, in a fun way, many aspects that make an ensemble successful. This happens whether the group is a recreational drum circle, group of school kids, or a corporate team. Drum circle games give individuals opportunities to showcase their abilities without needing to judge others or themselves, or compete. The drum circle is a great equalizer.

Who Uses The Games?

People use Rhythmical Alchemy Playshop games in many forums and in diverse ways:

- Facilitators of family friendly community drum circles incorporate RAP drum circle games into their events. These games direct the players' attention to aspects of their music making that help them connect more fully in their rhythm grooves.
- Hand drum teachers use RAP games to loosen up their students' playing before the real drum class starts. Some teachers also use the RAP games to reduce student-crisis-mode stress as they close the session.
- Music and school teachers use RAP games in their classroom to teach.
- Corporate trainers include RAP games in their rhythm-based experiential team-building formats.
- Conference keynote speakers sometimes use RAP games to break the ice with their audience at the beginning of their presentations.
- A few RAP graduates, who are conductors, are using the playshop games with their orchestras as warm-up exercises, to build ensemble consciousness in a new way.
- Many REMO Health Rhythms™ graduates are incorporating RAP games into the rhythm activities that they facilitate in hospitals and clinics, and among special needs populations.
- Kids-at-risk counselors who have graduated from my Village Music Circles™ training use RAP games in their programs in Australia, America and Europe.
- Drum groups that focus on culturally specific rhythms use RAP games to help fine tune their ensemble playing.
- Recreational drummers play the games as a way to create solid rhythm groove platforms for better group improvisation.

Groups that use Rhythmical Alchemy Playshop games run the gamut from prenatal classes to hospice communities.

The German Music Teachers

Modern Music School in Germany has 60 schools spread across the country, and they operate under the mandate that learning music should be fun. A few months before my annual European Facilitators' Playshop tour, the *Modern Music School* held a Teachers' Day. The opening session of the day was a drum circle facilitated by Till Willhousan, a VMC graduate. The 100 music teachers in attendance were asked, "Who would like to learn how to facilitate a drum circle?" 65 of them said yes, so I was asked to add a Facilitators' Training Playshop specifically for those music teachers during my stay in Germany.

An understanding of the universal principles of musicality is a basic foundation for a music teacher. In a typical 3-day VMC Facilitator Playshop, the players arrive with various levels of musical experience and understanding. Because it cannot be taught in a single weekend, I usually only point to musicality as it relates to what the participants need to acquire and understand in order to be good facilitators.

The program with these 65 music teachers from the Teachers' Day in Germany would be my first opportunity to do a Facilitators' Playshop exclusively for music teachers. From all of my facilitator programs during the European tours up until that time, only 44 music teachers and 84 drum teachers had graduated. With these 65 music teachers, musicality was a deep pool into which we would be able to dive and swim around for the whole weekend. I excitedly jumped at the chance!

Music teachers came from all over Germany to the Facilitators' Playshop in the old village of Idar-Oberstein nestled in the hills west of Frankfurt. Because all of the participants were teachers, I adapted the Playshop to meet their knowledge of musicality and their intention to incorporate drum circles and drum circle games into their curricula.

As in all of my Facilitator Playshop trainings, I assessed the demographics of the

attendees to better understand what populations they would be serving. It is unusual to have a group of all music teachers, so I asked them about their additional occupational associations. I read my list and they raised their hands if they were involved in that occupation. The 65 music teachers were also associated with the following vocations:
- 23 Drum Teachers
- 21 Professional Musicians
- 1 School Teacher
- 1 Music Therapist
- 1 Special Needs Professional
- 3 Infant-Toddler Facilitators
- 3 Medically Related Professionals

When I got to the bottom of my checklist I asked the group, "How many of you consider yourselves to be recreational drummers?" They did not understand the question. "What is a recreational drummer?" they asked. I explained that a recreational drummer is someone who drums

The German music teachers at the Playshop in the old village of Idar-Oberstein

just for fun, enjoyment and recreation. When I had established that they understood what a recreational drummer is, I asked the question again. Still no one raised their hand. "No one here drums for fun?!?" I asked, "Not even the drum teachers?"

Someone from the group stated, "It's a *job*." Not one of the German music teachers considered themselves to be a recreational drummer. Although I have been able to find music teachers in Germany who are also rhythmical evangelists, generally being a music teacher or drum teacher is explicitly a job in their culture.

In an informal circle at the close of the program I asked, "Now that you've experienced the Playshop, would you consider drumming with others for fun?" I was pleased to see that a third of the attendees raised their hands, with a smile and a laugh.

Spontaneous rhythmical spirit is in every child.

about these games

Instrument Combinations

Your drum circle orchestra needs to contain the variety of instruments that will produce the widest range of sounds possible. Whether your circle has an instrument combination of all membrane drums, all hand percussion, or a mixture of both, it is important that the circle contain many different timbres, pitches and tones. This will provide the best opportunity for your participants to express themselves fully, through rhythmical and musical interaction.

The Rhythmical Alchemy Playshop games in this volume are designed to be played with all drums, meaning that all of the players in the circle will be playing some sort of membrane drum. Most of these games can also be easily adapted for the participants to play hand percussion or a mixed combination of both drums and percussion instruments.

Ken Crampton

Isabelle Crampton playing her dad's low pitched Jun Juns.

All Drums

When everyone in the circle is playing some type of drum we call it all drums. When these instruments are struck, the long notes from their drum heads overlap each other, creating beautiful harmonic melody lines. The optimum combination of drums for musical improvisation is an equal mix of low, medium and high pitched membrane drums dispersed among the players. Variations in timbre can be created by using a combination of drumsticks, mallets, and hands on the drum heads.

Low Pitched Drum Examples

The large double-headed drums such as Brazilian surdos, drum set floor toms, and West African dunduns are typically the lowest-pitched drums in your circle. You can also use hand drums such as Cuban tumbas, Brazilian tan-tans, Ngoma drums from the Congo, and large frame drums as bottom drums.

In larger circles, I set up a sound bowl, or concentric circles of chairs, with my low drums in the center circle. I place the bass players around the inner circle so they can easily see and hear each other.

Kids playing at the St Catherine of Seina School for Destitute Children, an orphanage in Mumbai, India.

Medium Pitched Drum Examples

Almost all rhythmaculture drum families have medium-pitched drums, such as the Cuban conga, West African djembe, and Nigerian ashiko. Medium sized frame drums and Remo Festival Drums are also medium pitched. These drums typically define the character of the rhythm being played. When I set up a sound bowl or concentric circles of chairs, I check to be sure that the middle drums are placed throughout the circle.

High Pitched Drum Examples

Facilitators find a wide variety of high-pitched drums such as the Afro-Cuban quinto, Arabic dumbeck, African talking drum, bongos, small frame drums and tightly-strung djembes and ashikos in their circles. The high-pitched drum players create all kinds of interesting interactive dialogue and patterns. Sprinkle your high drums among the low and middle drums to add spice.

All Percussion

Instead of using membrane drums, players can use all hand percussion; that is, they can play bells, shakers and wood timbre instruments. Because each percussion note has a short duration, players create a very crisp, distinct and identifiable melody line when playing these instruments. Ideally they would use one third bells, one third shakers and one third wood instruments dispersed throughout the circle. Use a variety of types of instruments in each timbral category to vary the sounds, pitches and tones.

Bells

Bells come in many shapes and sizes of metal. Their timbre is the sharp sound of wood against metal, as we strike the bells with sticks. Their tone and pitch vary depending on their shape, size and thickness. Because the bell has the longest-lasting note of the hand percussion instruments, and due to the range of pitches in a group of bells, overlapping notes create harmonies inside the group song.

Examples of bells include agogo bells, small cow bells, and double bell gonkoques. You can add a special metal instrument such as a triangle, a Tibetan bell or a small gong for spice.

Shakers

Shakers come in many shapes and sizes, with containers typically made of gourds, plastic cylinders or tin cans. Sometimes the beads or seeds are inside the shaker container, and sometimes you find the beads or seeds strung on the outside of a gourd in a tied-macramé netting. Seed pod shakers have large wooden seeds loosely woven together. I also put tambourines without membrane heads in the shaker category because they are imprecise instruments that you shake to play, even though the jingles on most of them are made of metal. You play a shaker by shaking it.

The more variety of percussion the better.

Wood

Most wood instruments are struck or scraped with wooden drumsticks or timbale sticks. Various wooden instruments include wood blocks as well as Latin-American guiros, Cuban claves and the now-popular carved Vietnamese wooden frogs with ridges on their backs. Some modern-

An example of a mixed drum and percussion ensemble.

day "woodblock" sounds are produced from instruments constructed in plastic.

You can add a special wood sounding instrument such as bamboo Angklungs from Thailand, a wooden tone box, or pentatonic marimba notes.

Mixed Ensemble

Instead of using *only membrane* drums or *only* hand percussion, players can mix it up and use both – producing a mixed ensemble.

The wide range of pitches and timbres in a mixed ensemble offers the greatest diversity of sound and melody. For example, for a 30 person circle you could spread 5 of each pitch of drum, and 5 each of bells, shakers and woods among the circle. Mix the instruments so the same types are not placed next to each other for optimum orchestrational sound.

Run the Gamut

For some games, I advise music and school teachers who have enough different equipment and the time, to run the gamut of options. Play these games first in a circle with all percussion instruments, then immediately afterward with an all drum circle, and finally play with an ensemble of mixed instruments. The all percussion groove will emphasize the space between the notes, while the all drum sound accents the melody line created by the membrane drum heads, and the mixed ensemble underscores the musicality of a percussion orchestra.

Here is a list of games recommended for running the gamut.

- Layering in an Ensemble, page 70
- Groove By the Numbers, page 72
- Sculpting a Song, page 64
- Share Your Groove, page 92

Circle Sizes & Configurations

As the facilitator of drum circle games it is up to you to take responsibility for your physical circle of players. Before beginning the event or distributing instruments, you need to establish the circle by setting up the physical space with chairs.

For up to thirty players I recommend a single circle. If you place a larger group in a single circle, the distance can create a rhythmical and visual disconnect between players across the circle. The sound arrives a fraction of a second later on the far side of the circle and the acoustical interaction between players can become sloppy. Then it becomes more of a challenge for you as facilitator to help maintain a solid steady group groove. A lot of your facilitation of the games can be done from your seat when you have thirty players or less.

For more than thirty players I set up concentric circles to place the participants in close playing proximity. For example, if I have thirty-six participants I set up two concentric seating circles with sixteen players in the inner circle, and twenty players in the outer circle. Then I make an aisle between each group of four seats in the inner circle, providing four aisles for access to the center of the circle.

Types of Games

The three types of games offered in Rhythmical Alchemy Playshops are agreement games, facilitated games and orchestrational games. Some of these games are also good groove starters and are listed below.

Three Types of RAP Games

Agreement Games

The game facilitator sets up specific parameters and rules for how a particular game is to be played, and gets the agreement of all the players involved. Then the game begins without any overt action by the facilitator. I refer to this type of game as an agreement game.

Examples:
- Passing the Note Game, page 47
- Passing the Rumble, page 48
- Passing Patterns, page 48
- Play What You Feel, page 50
- Call and Response to Groove, page 54
- Layering in a Rhythm, page 67
- Layering Rhythm Dialogue, page 68
- Layering in an Ensemble, page 70
- Evolution From the Mixed Pile, page 82
- Groove to Solo Game, page 100

- Call to Solo Game, page 104
- Share Your Groove, page 92
- Drum Groove By Pitch, page 96

Facilitated Games

When the game facilitator must overtly run the game by counting for the group or giving directions to the group as the game progresses, I call it a facilitated game.

Examples:
- Groove By the Numbers, Beginner Version, page 74
- Groove By the Numbers, Intermediate Version, page 76
- Evolution to Timbre Game, page 84
- Ensemble Evolution Game, page 88
- Blind Date Orchestra Game, page 89
- Clap It to the Drum, page 56
- Clave-Clap-to-Drum-Circle-Song Game, page 58
- Air Drumming to Groove, page 60

Orchestrational Games

For orchestrational games, players take turns being in charge of specific facilitation responsibilities during the execution of that particular game. The participant who is orchestrating usually stands in the center, except for small circles of 8 or less players, when they can direct from their seat.

Examples:
- Call to Groove Game, page 42
- Rumble Wave Game, page 44
- Rumble Point Game, page 45
- Selecting a Specific Orchestra, page 90
- Musical Chairs Evolution, page 80
- Sculpting a Song, page 64
- Share Your Groove on the Run, page 94

Groove Starters

Several of the drum circle games in this volume are great groove starters for recreational drumming circles. These games can help your drum circle create unique rhythm grooves that will be sustainable and "groovy."

The accompanying DVD also includes a few short vignettes. In the Groove Starter section are some examples of how a game facilitator might start or stop a group groove.

Platforms For Learning

Platform for learning is the idea of offering a series of games in a sequentially progressive order of complexity and sophistication. Each game is an experiential learning platform that teaches a basic playing element that when learned, enables the participants to successfully complete the game. Each of these successes prepares players to be ready to play the next game in the series. The first game teaches the most basic elements. Then the players will be able to use those elements in the more sophisticated second and third games in the series.

The call and response games (page 49), the layering games (page 66), and the groove by the numbers games (page 72) described in this volume are examples of platforms for learning.

Not all rhythm bliss happens on a drum.

Orchestrational Techniques

This section describes some of the orchestrational techniques that you can use to facilitate RAP drum circle games. Learn how to start a group groove with a call to groove, gain the attention of a everyone playing in a circle with an attention call, and bring the group to a rhythmical stop with a rumble, a call and response, or a stop cut. Read about how to sculpt a circle too.

Call to Groove

Call to groove is a way to start a group rhythm, from no one playing to everyone in the circle starting to play at the same time. To call to groove, vocally count the group into a groove while physically marking the pulse as a model. "One, two, let's all play" is one vocal version of call to groove. When you do this it is helpful to the players if you set the pulse and pace of the upcoming groove with your voice, your body and your musical instrument before the call. You want to start each rhythm with minimum cacophony and maximum congruency among the players.

The group will almost always make rhythmical adjustments during the first few measures after you start the groove, but there are ways to minimize the adjustment they must make after each individual player starts their own independent rhythm on the same first beat. Counting the first two pulses "one, two" and then using the last two pulses in the starting measure of "Let's all play" to verbally indicate where to start playing does not always give participants enough time to be ready to play. Prepare your group rhythmically using your voice and body language before you lead a call to groove. Otherwise, you will almost always put some, or most, of your circle into crisis mode, especially if it is the group's first drum circle experience.

A few tricks can make the call to groove less of a surprise and a lot smoother, with less adjustment needed after the first note:

- Play a pulse on a cow bell, starting at least one cycle before your count to groove. Continue playing the pulse on the bell as you count and after the group starts. Marking the pulse helps lock in the groove for the players. Don't worry. Keep smiling.
- Step in time at the pace at which you want the rhythm to start.
- Prepare the group for the call to groove by speaking to them at the pace at which you want the rhythm to start.

With your voice you count the first two pulses and between the 3rd and 4th pulse, you vocally encourage the group to start to play. Say the words *one* and *two*, as well as *let's* and *play* on the pulse of the rhythm. Say the word *all* between the 3rd and 4th pulses.

count	1	2	3	4	1
pulse	I	I	I	I	I
call	one	two	Let's all Play		Start groove

"One, two, let's all play" is a standard call to groove. More examples:

- "One, two, start your groove"
- "One, two, share your Spirit"
- "One, two, start to play"
- "One, two, make-up your-own"
- "One, two, you-know-what-to-do"

The Call to Groove Game described on page 42 is a great way to empower your circle as they start playing together. Additional ways to start a group groove, for game facilitators:

- Clap or play the pulse on a bell or block and invite everyone to join in with their own rhythm

- Ask one of the participants to start a rhythm and be prepared to reinforce it. Invite the other players to join in the fun.

Attention Call

Attention calls are body signals that gain the group's attention and let them know that a new facilitation signal is about to be given. These calls are typically given by the facilitator when the group is in full groove. In some situations you can use vocal calls to help reinforce the body language attention call signal.

There are many types of attention calls for facilitating a community drum circle but for the purposes of these drum circle games we need only one type: the full group attention call. You do this by simply holding up your hand with your index finger pointing to the sky while vocally getting the group's attention. Don't forget to make eye contact and smile!

Stop Cut

A stop cut is a powerful drum circle facilitation body language tool that can be used with the full playing group, sections of the group or with individual players.

There are many ways to execute a stop cut and there are many stop cut styles created by different drum circle facilitators. For the RAP games I use, as my body language stop cut signal, the safe signal used in baseball by the umpires.

Give the stop cut signal on the first pulse of any given rhythm cycle. By giving a full group attention call and then giving a full group stop cut you are often able to stop the circle's music on a dime.

Call and Response

The actions of call and response games are simple. Someone does something and everyone repeats it. For example, one of the players in the circle plays a pattern that fits within a one measure rhythmical cycle. I include call and response games in this volume, starting on page 49.

Rumble

A rumble is a simple orchestrational tool that initiates and controls rhythm chaos. You can initiate a rumble sound in your group of players by holding your hands out in front of you and wiggling them quickly from the wrists. The group responds by creating musical chaos, a non-rhythmical noise, with their instruments. Participants create a rumble by playing notes as fast as possible, on their drum, bells, wood blocks or shakers. It is that simple, and everyone loves it!

When participants are orchestrating rumbles in the center of the circle, time can disappear due to the fun that they're having and they can exhaust their drummers because rumbling is aerobic. As facilitator, you can orchestrate a sixty second continuous rumble before beginning the games so your players will understand just how long a minute can be when they are playing fast notes repeatedly. This can help players understand why each person's turn is only thirty to sixty seconds when they're orchestrating rumbles.

Sculpting

Sculpting is the action of selecting and identifying a person, a group, a drum type or a timbre in order to give specific facilitation direction to that group. That action prepares whomever you have sculpted to react to the upcoming direction. You give a sculpting signal when you plan to give that person or group another signal, while your event is in full groove.

When you want a selected group of players to continue playing while you stop cut others in the circle, you can give a continue-to-play signal. The standard continue-to-play body language signal is to point your two index fingers toward each other in front of your chest and rotate them around each other.

For the Sculpting a Song Game on page 64, participants take turns selecting and showcasing an ensemble in the drum circle by sculpting several individual players who continue to play while others stop. Some Volume Two games will include sculpting by sections.

The accompanying DVD shows examples of me, as game facilitator, vocally sculpting full group percussion timbres or drum pitches for educational purposes. Simply by watching the video you can learn how to use these techniques when you are the game facilitator.

Below are descriptions of two sculpting scenarios that you can find on the DVD.

- In example number three in the "What is Sculpting" section of the DVD, while the group was in full groove, I sculpted to showcase all of the low drum players, then gradually built the full groove again.
  - First I showcased all of the low drum players by giving them a "continue to play" signal, and immediately giving a "stop cut" signal to the rest of the players. This revealed the low drum song to the non-playing participants.
  - I then adjusted the low drum song by asking the showcased players to "listen to each other and take out one 'not important' note" from their rhythmic pattern. Once the extra notes were removed, we had a more solidified low drum groove.
  - I then layered in those who were playing instruments with mallets, inviting them to join into the low drum song.
  - Then I invited all players of bells, shakers and wood blocks to join the groove.
  - Finally I invited all the hand drummers to add their contributions to the rhythm mix.
- In the Ensemble Evolution Game example found in the "Evolution from the Tray" section of the DVD, after we evolved from all drums to all percussion, I sculpted by timbre.
  - First I showcased the bell players by verbally telling them to "continue to play," and stop cut the rest of the players.
  - With just the bells playing I verbally prepared the players for a "timbre switch" letting the bell players know that they will stop and the shakers will start at the same time on my signal.
  - After I gave the "switch" signal, only the shakers were being played.
  - Then I layered in the wood block players using the words "at your leisure, come on in."

- Finally I counted in the bell players, so that everyone was playing their instrument.

All the actions taken above were different forms of sculpting.

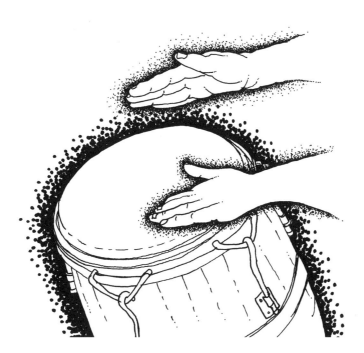

games

Too Much Drumming?

I have adapted the Rhythmical Alchemy Playshop programs (RAP) to meet the needs of different professional populations throughout the world.

For graduates of my Drum Circle Facilitation Playshops, we present the *Facilitators Rhythmical Alchemy Playshop* (FRAP) to help them adapt certain RAP games to be presented in their rhythm events.

I have also presented many experiential training RAP game programs to corporate facilitators and trainers, called a *Corporate Rhythmical Alchemy Playshop* (CRAP).

When a particular community of veteran recreational drummers in Bergen, Norway asked me to come and do an all *Drumming Rhythmical Alchemy Playshop* (DRAP), I was happy to meet their needs.

They wanted only drum circle games without any other RAP games that would include vocals, hand percussion, movement, etc. They wanted me to present different ways to sit and drum together that would improve their musicality and rhythmical expertise. So I put together a full weekend of drum circle games, many of which are represented in this book.

A typical Rhythmical Alchemy Playshop program starts on a Friday afternoon, goes all day Saturday, and runs until late afternoon on Sunday. At the Norway DRAP, by Saturday afternoon the participants had experienced over 8 hours of drum circle games, with 8 more hours of drumming to go.

After a short tea break on Saturday afternoon, some representatives of the group came up to me and said that many of the players' hands hurt from so much drumming. The group requested that I include some of my other RAP games that did not require hitting drums.

So I turned the DRAP into a RAP with a variety of many types of interactive rhythm games, including hand drum games.

Orchestrational Teaching Games

Some of the methods you use to facilitate a community drum circle are the same as those needed for the games in this book. The orchestrational teaching games I describe in this section guide the process of learning facilitation techniques for both you as the game facilitator and your players in the circle. By playing these games you will learn ways to facilitate the drum circle games.

Learn how to start a group groove with a call to groove, gain the attention of everyone playing in a circle with an attention call, and bring the group to a rhythmical stop with a rumble, a call and response, or a stop cut. By playing these simple orchestrational games in your circle of friends, with kids at school, or at a community drum circle you can empower them to self facilitate.

Call to Groove Game

Call to Groove is one of the first exercises that I do in the Village Music Circles™ playshops for drum circle facilitators. By using this exercise as a game in your drum circle, everyone in the circle will learn to recognize the orchestrational signals, and how to respond to them. At the same time, players will learn how to use the signals themselves.

Each person takes turns starting the rhythm circle by doing the call to groove. Depending on the size of the group and the time available, the game facilitator can either invite a few volunteers to take turns starting a group groove, or ask everyone who is comfortable playing the game to take turns — one after another according to their seating arrangement.

Play the Game

- Before anyone starts playing, the selected starter goes to the center of the circle.

- The starter plays a pulse at their selected pace for at least one measure and then initiates their call to groove.

- While playing the pulse, the starter says "one, two, let's all play."

- The group responds by beginning to play on the next pulse.

- After the group grooves for a few cycles, you want the rhythm to stop in preparation for the next participant's turn. The starter (or if you are working with smaller kids, you as the game facilitator) has choices for how to stop the groove. Either make an attention call and then a stop cut, or call out with both voice and hands at the same time for a group rumble. The rumble stops the groove and creates a celebratory cacophony of joyful noise. To stop the group rumble, the starter makes a stop cut.

When this game is played in a small circle, the starter can orchestrate the group while sitting in their seat. The person who is facilitating the closing rumble raises their hands high in the air at the end of the rumble and when they bring them down on top of their drum, everyone plays their last note.

- After the stop cut, silence follows and it is now the next person's turn to do a call to groove at a tempo different than the one used by the person before them.

To keep the game simple for a group of younger kids, you as the game facilitator can invite each participant to come into the center of the circle to signal the call to groove or the stop cut.

- Start the groove for the circle from your seat, and invite the participant to do a stop cut and then sit down. Then you can do another call to groove and invite the next participant to do a group stop cut.

  or

- Invite the participant to do the call to groove and go back to their seat while the circle of participants play the rhythm. Then you do the stop cut from your seat and invite the next participant to start a new group groove from the center of the circle.

Rumble Wave Game

Participants enjoy orchestrating the Rumble Wave Game. When the players in the circle respond to the signals, it builds confidence for the orchestrator and teaches the whole group about volume dynamics. Even very young children can play this easy game.

Play the Game

- Orchestrators of the rumble wave game start while the circle of participants is not playing. When it is their turn, each person comes to the center of the circle and initiates a rumble sound among the players by holding their hands out in front and wiggling them quickly from the wrists.

- The whole circle of players responds by creating musical chaos, a non-rhythmical noise, with their instruments.

- Then by raising or lowering their hands as they give the rumble signal, the initiator is able to raise and lower the volume of the group's rumble, thus creating rumble waves.

- The initiator makes a stop cut to end the rumble. Allow each circle participant thirty to sixty seconds per turn.

Rumble Point Game

The Rumble Point Game teaches about pitches, drum circle song consciousness, and builds confidence.

In some cultures pointing is an aggressive disrespectful act. I teach my RAP game participants how to do what I call the "Disneyland point" by extending my hand, with my fingers closed and my palm up, toward them. With preschoolers, I let them do it any way they know how to point.

Play the Game

- Orchestrators of the rumble point game start while the circle of participants is not playing. When it is their turn, the designated pointer comes to the center of the circle, or for small circles they can orchestrate from their seat. Each turn lasts for thirty to sixty seconds.

- Players rumble on their instruments anytime the pointer points to them, and stop playing when the pointer stops pointing toward them.

- By pointing to anyone in the circle for any length of time, and sequentially pointing to as many different people as they choose, the pointer creates a rumble song. Every song will be different.

The rumble group pointing game is a variation of the rumble point game. Instead of pointing to a single player, the orchestrator holds out both hands to encompass two, three or four players sitting next to each other. Those participants rumble until the orchestrator redirects their hands to another group of players in the circle.

Passing Games

These simple games are a great way to do team building with any age group. They require that players pay attention to the circle as a whole as well as to the person next to them. All of the passing games naturally encourage peripheral vision and peripheral hearing in the participants. Participants pass a note, a rumble, or a pattern around the circle from one player to the next, and everyone stays in their seats.

Passing the Note Game

One of the most simple drum circles games is to have each player in turn play one note on their instrument and, in turn, pass that note around the circle. Before starting the Passing the Note Game, remind the participants to listen to the different songs that this game can create. Passing a note around the circle creates a simple drum circle song that changes with each note.

Play the Game

- The first person initiates the passing the note game by playing a single note while the circle of participants is not playing.
- The next person to the right immediately strikes their instrument.
- Then the next person strikes their note, and the next, and the next... as the note gets passed around the circle.

Variations

- Send the note around the opposite direction and listen to the new song.
- After passing a note around the circle a few cycles, measure the number of seconds of the passing the note song from start to finish. Challenge the group to work together to complete the song in a shorter amount of time. Ask the participants for strategies that would accomplish their goal.
- Ask every other person to play a note as the song goes around the circle. If you have an uneven number of people, the song will spiral and include everyone within two rounds. If you have an even number of people in the circle then instruct the players who have already played to wait a round before playing again. The song then hops over the set of people who most recently played.

Passing the Rumble

The Passing the Rumble Game starts while the circle of participants is not playing. One person rumbles for one to two seconds, and then stops. Then the person next to them rumbles, and the next and the next until the rumble has been passed from player to player all the way around the circle. Change the direction the rumble is passed and you will create a whole new passing the rumble song.

Passing Patterns

Passing Patterns is a more sophisticated passing game for drum circle players. Instead of passing one note, the players in the circle pass a one measure pattern. An example of a measure is a single cycle of 4 beats.

Play the Game

- The first person plays a one measure pattern on their instrument while the circle of participants is not playing. They then stop playing.
- At the first pulse of the next cycle the next player plays their own single measure pattern.
- Then the next person plays their unique pattern, and the next, and the next... as the pattern song gets passed around the circle.
- The game facilitator can play the pulse on a bell or wood block to support a smooth pattern exchange among beginning groups of players.

Call & Response Games

The actions of call and response games are simple. Someone does something and everyone repeats it. For example, one of the players in the circle plays a pattern that fits within a one measure rhythmical cycle. All the players in the circle listen to that person's call and on the first note of the next rhythmical cycle they respond to the pattern called, usually by playing the same pattern. Participants take turns calling and responding, with everyone staying in their seats. With beginning-beginner players, staying within a single measure is not the goal. Exact duplication is not required in any of the call and response games in the Rhythmical Alchemy Playshop series.

In formal music education, Echo is a specific teaching activity in which the responders are expected to reproduce the call pattern as closely as possible. In call and response drum circle games I encourage players to respond to the call with any pattern with which they feel comfortable. Even though the actions of call and response games appear to be like those used for Echo, the intention and expected results of these actions differ. With Echo there are many ways to play the pattern, but only one of these ways is completely correct. In call and response games there are many ways for the players to respond correctly and only one incorrect way – that is, to not respond at all, and even that is all right in some situations. Remember that it is important to encourage rhythmical empowerment and improvisation when you facilitate these games rather than expecting participants to play correctly.

Expect anything from your players in call and response, from vocals to body movements in rhythmical combination with anything played on the drum.

Play What You Feel

I created Play What You Feel as a name introduction game for kids. It is a fun and effective ice breaker for everybody and encourages self expression. With this game, the facilitator invites the player making the call to say their first name and then use their instrument to express their feelings in a short burst of sound – not necessarily a rhythmical pattern.

As game facilitator you encourage the players to express themselves. They can make any noise they want on their instrument, not necessarily of a rhythmical nature or within a specifically counted measure. I refer to this as a non-time-signature-specific call and response game. Participants can express how they feel by scratching the head of their drum with their fingernails, hitting only one note, making a short rumble or any other sound. You can take away any performance pressure a participant may have by telling them that they do not need to play something musical or rhythmical.

Play the Game

- With no one playing, a person says their first name and then immediately plays what they feel on their instrument.
- The group responds by repeating the person's name and then reproducing the instrument call as well as they can using their instruments.

It is that simple.

The Basic Call and Response Game

This Basic Call and Response Game invites participants to express themselves within a specific time frame, and to explore rhythmical phrasing using one measure patterns. You as game facilitator want to encourage the players to keep it simple. This drum circle game is more about sharing rhythmical spirit than about showcasing individual drumming expertise.

Play the Game

- With no one playing, a participant in the drum circle makes a call on their instrument, playing whatever one measure pattern they want.
- All of the other players respond to the call on the first note of the next measure by repeating the pattern on their instruments.
- At the start of the next measure after the group response, the person sitting to the right of the last caller becomes the new caller and plays their unique one measure pattern.
- Again, the other players respond to the call on the first note of the next measure by repeating the pattern on their instruments.
- The game continues with each person taking a turn calling, and with the circle responding, until all the players in the circle have made a call.

Facilitating Specific Groups of Players

Groups have different needs depending on their level of experience as players.

In a young kids' circle it is more about sharing their rhythm than learning how to stay within a defined measure of time, so it is not necessary for each call to start on the next pulse after the group has responded to the last call. Simply let each person do their call and the group give the response, with no need to enforce a metronomic pace.

With 5th through 8th grade students, or for a mixed age group, the facilitator can play a pulse on a bell to help keep time while encouraging the caller to start on the first pulse of the next rhythmical cycle. I like to play the first pulse on the lip of the cow bell to emphasize the one and then play the second, third, and fourth pulses on the top of the bell for a lighter sound. Donk dink dink dink Donk dink dink dink... If they miss starting their pattern on the one, I keep playing the pulse, and tell them it is all right to miss the start and to wait for the start of the next measure. I use body language to help them start on the next one. Remember to keep an attitude of empowering your players and avoid adding performance pressure.

In a recreational drumming circle, the game can also be played with each player doing a pre-designated number of call and response sequences for each turn. For instance, a player makes three calls and the group responds three times before the next person takes their three-call turn.

John Fitzgerald, left, facilitating call and response patterns with a cow bell in Hong Kong

Call & Response Oops!

While playing the call and response game with an all-hand-percussion ensemble, one of the participants began a call on his cow bell for the group, but with his first strike he knocked the bell out of his hand with his stick. While attempting to catch the bell before it fell to the floor, he also dropped his stick. When his stick and bell came crashing to the floor, the group's immediate spontaneous response was to toss all of their percussion instruments onto the floor as well. One great big rumbling crash ensued, along with a great big group belly laugh – the perfect response.

Call and Response to Groove

Once the group learns the basic call and response game, they can use it as a platform for the more sophisticated interaction offered in Call and Response to Groove. This game teaches improvisation based on a set pattern that starts the groove.

Play the Game

- With no one playing, a participant in the drum circle plays a pattern encompassing one measure.

- At the first note of the next measure the group responds to that pattern, reproducing it on their instrument.

- The group continues to repeat the call pattern until their playing solidifies into a continuous drum circle groove.

- Once a group establishes their groove, the game facilitator invites individual players to improvise using the basic call pattern as a foundation.

- Either enjoy this interactive musical drum circle groove until the group explores the groove completely and is ready to stop, or bring the groove to a close and select a volunteer to make a call to start a new groove.

- After playing this game two or three times, participants will start improvising on their own, without needing an invitation from a facilitator.

This game is a great groove starter for recreational drummers and drum circle enthusiasts.

Put-It-on-the-Drum Games

I designed Put-It-on-the-Drum Games to create starting patterns with a minimal number of notes, leaving space to help make the beginning of a groove clean and simple. Participants create simple rhythm patterns vocally, by clapping patterns with their hands, or by playing in the air before they put it on the drum. The patterns become simple rhythm platforms that are improvisation friendly.

When a facilitator calls a group to groove, "One, two, let's all play," the participants all start without knowing what patterns others in the circle are going to play. Then, as they begin to drum and listen to each other, they must "sort out the groove by committee." What they sort out as they play is what I call the "drum circle song." Depending on a group's listening and playing expertise they must play for a few measures, up to as much as a few minutes, before a coherent song emerges. A drum circle song usually emerges more quickly for an experienced recreational ensemble than for a community drum circle full of first time players.

Use these games to create more space in players' patterns. Then when they start the groove together, the patterns they play will merge into a drum song in a simpler fashion than by committee and in a shorter time period.

Busy rhythm patterns have lots of notes with little space between them. These crowded patterns are not improvisation friendly. Simple patterns cause less adjustment chaos as the drum song emerges. By playing these put-it-on-the-drum games, participants learn to leave more space in their playing for listening and improvisation.

Clap It to the Drum

The Clap It to the Drum Game educates the players in your circle about the importance of listening and dialogue, and is a great way to start a simple, clean and solid groove. The game facilitator plays a pulse on a bell or wood block while encouraging players to clap patterns and listen to each other, before they start to play their drums. Once a hand-clapping groove is established, the facilitator calls the group to groove on their drums.

When playing with hands on a drum it is easy to create busy rhythm patterns full of notes spaced closely together. It is hard, though, to clap a pattern with lots of closely spaced notes. When players clap their simple patterns together before putting them on their drums, they create a collaborative starting groove that leaves room for more listening, more space between each player's notes, and more room to improvise.

Play the Game

- Everyone sits in front of their drum in a circle.

- While playing the pulse on a bell or wood block, the game facilitator invites the players to start by clapping any rhythm they like.

- Once the group is in full clap groove, the game facilitator encourages them to adjust their clapping rhythms while listening to the group groove.

- The facilitator then gives the special call to groove signal that invites the players to put their hand-clapping rhythms on their drums.

Instead of saying

I	•	I	•	I	•	I	•
One		Two		Let's	All	Play	

The facilitator says

I	•	I	•	I	•	I	•
One		Two		Put It	On the	Drum	

and the drum groove starts.

- The facilitator encourages the players to listen to the groove and add or subtract notes to contribute to the collaborative drum song.

- The players enjoy their drum circle song until the facilitator brings the groove to a close.

When working with a group of young children it helps when the game facilitator continues to play a pulse on a bell or wood block as players switch from clapping to drumming. This pulse helps solidify their groove.

This game is a great groove starter for recreational drummers and drum circle enthusiasts.

Clave-Clap-to-Drum-Circle-Song Game

In the Clave-Clap-to-Drum-Circle-Song Game the facilitator teaches a simple pattern for players to use while they start a foundational groove. Everyone in the circle claps a clave pattern together, and then they listen and improvise around the pattern while still clapping. By altering their clapping patterns, players are able to listen to the overall rhythm without being distracted by drum pitches and timbres. This game offers a new way to start a solid groove to a magical drum song.

Play the Game

- Players are ready with their drums in front of them, and the game facilitator claps the clave pattern with the group.

```
I   •   I   •   I   •   I   •
X   X   •   X   •   X   X   •
```

- Once the group is in full clave clap groove, the facilitator encourages them to improvise their own clapping rhythm while listening to the group.
- The facilitator reminds the participants to listen to everyone and play around each others' patterns.
- The facilitator calls to groove in four counts, "One, two, put it on the drum."
- The participants put their clapping patterns on the drum.
- The group listens to their drum circle song as they play together.

Any simple pattern with five or less notes will work. Make the pattern uncomplicated with minimal syncopation. Simpler patterns offer more space for individual improvisation. This game is a great groove starter for recreational drummers and drum circle enthusiasts.

Air Drumming to Groove

The Air Drumming to Groove Game helps players merge into a groove that begins with everyone playing simple rhythm patterns. The game facilitator encourages participants to air play, above their drums, whatever rhythms they like. Then they sculpt out notes before playing the patterns on the drums. This game teaches drum circle participants how to start a groove with simplified rhythm patterns that merge gracefully into a drum circle song.

Play the Game

- Players in the circle hold their drums, prepared to play them.

- The facilitator plays the pulse on a cowbell, emphasizing the "one" on the lip of the bell and playing the other pulses on the top surface of the bell, and directs the participants to each play a pattern in the air just above their drum.

- Players imagine the sounds of the patterns they are playing while they air drum.

- As facilitator, you instruct each participant to remove the least important note in their pattern as they continue to play in the air.

- After a few more cycles of air drumming, the facilitator asks players to each remove the most expendable note still in their hand pattern, thus simplifying their rhythm even more. This creates more space so that when the players start the groove, all the patterns will merge in a clean simple fashion.

- The facilitator calls to groove in four counts, "One, two, put it on the drum" and the players place their patterns on their drums.

- The group now has a basic rhythmical foundation for musical improvisation.

- As the group groove solidifies, the game facilitator invites players to listen to their rhythmical and musical relationship to the other players and add or subtract notes for a positive contribution to the overall musical collaboration.

This game is a great groove starter for recreational drummers and drum circle enthusiasts.

Facilitators can run the gamut of instrumentation with this game, using all hand percussion instruments, and then a mixed ensemble. Bell and wood block players will each hold their instrument in one hand and play in the air above the instrument with a stick. Shaker players place their instruments in their laps and play in the air as if they were holding them. Then they each pick up their shaker and play when called to groove.

Play My Name Game

The Play My Name Game uses the vocalized syllables of a person's name as the foundational rhythm for a drum circle groove. This is an introduction to learning by listening and then singing a vocal rhythm before playing the pattern on the drum. Teachers can use this game to set a foundation for singing rhythm patterns before playing them. Players experience the truth in an old African adage, "If you can sing it, you can play it."

The groove originator sings their name in a rhythmical fashion and the other participants chime in by singing the same pattern. Most first names have a limited number of syllables. For more variety, the game facilitator can ask players to say their whole names. Each syllable acts as an accent point when pronounced. These accent points define spots-in-time for a player to naturally strike their instrument when they use the sounds of the name as a rhythm model.

Many games are naturally played using 4/4 time signatures, but some peoples' names lend themselves to being sung and played in triplet time, depending on how a person sings the rhythm. For example:

4/4 time

I	•	•	•	I	•	•	•	I	•	•	•	I	•	•	•
Ar		Thur		Hull				Ar		Thur		Hull			

Triplet time

I	•	•	I	•	•	I	•	•	I	•	•
Ar			Thur Hull			Ar			Thur Hull		

Play the Game

- With no one playing, a participant sings their first name in a rhythmical fashion and immediately plays their name in the same rhythm on their instrument.

- The group responds by singing the person's name in the same rhythm and immediately plays the name in the same rhythm on their instruments.

- The next person sings their name in rhythm and immediately plays their rhythm name on their instrument.

- The group responds by rhythmically singing the person's name, then playing it.

- The game continues until everyone's name has been sung and played.

As a conclusion, the facilitator can choose someone to sing their name in rhythm and invite the other participants to play an ongoing groove based on that person's name.

Jung Jin Lei

While doing a RAP with music therapists in Seoul, South Korea, I attempted to facilitate the Play My Name game.

As I discovered, the complete names of many Koreans consists of three names, each name being one syllable. Here are some examples from the Playshop: Jee Won Yoon, Seong Hwan Ahn and Jung Jin Lei.

That meant when we played the "Play My Name" game, everyone would say their three syllable name and then hit their drum three times as the call. The rest of the participants would then respond by hitting their drums three times.

Name, Boom Boom Boom, Group Response, Boom Boom Boom, Next name, Boom Boom Boom, Group Response, Boom Boom Boom, and so on.

Everyone playing their three syllables was not enough variety for teaching phraseology in rhythm, so I had to stop the name game and teach "Play What You Feel" instead.

I learned that not all games are appropriate for all cultures.

Sculpting a Song

Sculpting a Song is a very useful and malleable orchestrational game that fits into its own category.

Sculpting a Song Game

Sculpting a Song is an orchestrational game in which the game facilitator offers participants an opportunity to stand in the middle of a drum circle in full groove and orchestrate. Selecting and showcasing a few players from within the larger circle unveils the selected participants and the unique drum song that they are playing.

Orchestrators are able to listen and discover rhythmical interactions, dialogues and harmonies created by specific players across the circle. They can then use their new awareness of these elements to improve their listening and interactive playing after they return to their seat.

Before beginning, the game facilitator explains how to orchestrate. "Sculpt a song by choosing participants around the circle, making eye contact with the person who you would like to sculpt. Give them the Disneyland point by extending your hand, with your fingers closed and your palm up, toward them. Give the selected players a continue-to-play signal. Stop cut the remaining players to unveil your song."

Depending on the size of the group and the time available, the game facilitator can either invite a few volunteers to take turns orchestrating, or ask everyone who is comfortable playing the game to take turns, one after another according to their seating arrangement.

Facilitators can run the gamut of instrumentation with this game when they work with students, using all drums, then all hand percussion instruments, and then a mixed ensemble.

Play the Game

- The game facilitator starts the circle with a call to groove and demonstrates the game by being the first orchestrator.

- Then the facilitator selects a volunteer to orchestrate.

- While the group is in full groove the orchestrator steps into the center of the circle. They listen to the rhythm song, sculpt several players, and give them the continue-to-play signal.

- Then the orchestrator gives an attention call to the whole group and signals the players, who are not selected, with a stop cut.

- These players stop playing and listen to the song that the orchestrator has sculpted.

- The orchestrator listens to and enjoys their song from the center of the circle for a few musical cycles.

- Then the orchestrator signals a call to groove, or just raises their hands above their head, and the non-playing participants join the new song.

- The orchestrator returns to their seat and a new volunteer orchestrator takes a turn.

When an orchestrator uses all of their senses to obtain all the information possible in their drum circle, they discover the beauty of musical rhythms, dialogues and harmonies.

Layering Games

Layering games emphasize listening and collaborative rhythm making. One player starts a rhythm and the participants listen and join the rhythm, one at a time. With their complementary contributions, they build a music ensemble.

The length of time for a specific groove is determined by the intentions of the event and needs of the age group. If the event timing is tightly structured you as facilitator may choose to control when each groove ends. For school kids the intention is often to provide as many different groove experiences as possible within the time available. With a larger group, the facilitator will need to select volunteers because there will not be enough time for every player to start a groove. By choosing volunteers sitting randomly in different places in the circle instead of going in order around the circle every player has a more equal chance of being the one to start a groove.

Recreational drumming groups enjoy starting a groove and then playing for the fullness of the groove instead of starting and stopping many times.

For over 20 years, a group of people affiliated with the Earth Drum Council in the Boston area have been doing a layering in a rhythm type of drum circle game. They call the game Round Robin. One of the elements they use in the game is person-to-person eye contact. The person who has last layered in makes eye contact with the person next to them as a signal to let that person know that the first player is fully engaged in the rhythm and the next person can start. This same process works when the group is done with the game and they start layering out person by person.

Layering in a Rhythm

Layering in a Rhythm is a basic groove starter that invites the participants to synchronize and synergize their playing.

Play the Game

- Designate a starting player. While no one is playing, that person starts the rhythm song.

- The person to the left of the starting player listens to the rhythm and then adds whatever rhythm they think would be appropriate to support and harmonize with the song being played.

- The person to the left of the second player listens to the two players, and then adds their complementary rhythm.

- The next person in turn listens to the song being created and plays their rhythmical contribution.

- This process continues until each player in the circle has layered their complementary part into the composition, creating a complete rhythm song.

- After everyone joins the rhythm and enjoys the composition for a while, the person who started the rhythm makes an attention call, shouts "Rumble!" and leads the groove to a close.

- The next volunteer starts a rhythm and continues this game. With a small group, you can take turns until everyone has had a chance to start a rhythm. No two songs will be the same.

I advise music and school teachers to run the gamut of possibilities with an all percussion circle first, then immediately afterward with an all drum circle, and finally with an ensemble of mixed instruments.

This game is a great groove starter for recreational drummers and drum circle enthusiasts.

Layering Rhythm Dialogue

The Layering Rhythm Dialogue Game directs players' attention to their fellow participants across the circle and encourages a musical conversation between them. Two players sitting across from each other start a rhythm dialogue. Players take turns layering in, back and forth across the circle. This process produces two playing ensembles sitting across from each other. As more participants join the groove, the two groups grow and merge into one drum circle ensemble.

Play the Game

- Designate a participant who starts the rhythm song as the first player in the drum circle.

- The person sitting directly across the circle listens to the rhythm and adds a pattern that supports, harmonizes or complements it.

- Next, after listening to the song being created by the two players across the circle from each other, the person sitting to the left of the first player adds their rhythmical contribution and becomes a member of Ensemble One.

- The fourth participant, who is sitting to the left of the single player across the circle from Ensemble One, contributes to the growing musical dialogue, and creates Ensemble Two with the person sitting next to them.

- This process of taking turns continues until every player in the circle has layered their rhythmical contributions into the composition. When all of the participants are playing together, then the two ensembles merge into one rhythm song.

This game is a great groove starter for recreational drummers and drum circle enthusiasts.

Layering in an Ensemble

The Layering in an Ensemble Game helps players develop their awareness of the importance of individual contributions to a rhythm. This game begins the same way as the Layering in a Rhythm Game. Then, as players continue to layer in, the first players who started the groove sequentially stop playing after a set number of participants are playing, so the ensemble moves around the circle. As players enter and leave the groove, the participants are able to appreciate the evolving song of the moving ensemble. It is as engaging to listen quietly as to actively play during this game.

The first six players of this game begin exactly as they would for the Layering in a Rhythm Game. Then, when six players are drumming, the first player will fade and the seventh player will join the ensemble.

Play the Game

- Designate a starting player. While no one is playing, that person starts the rhythm song.

- The person to the left of the starting player listens to the rhythm and then adds whatever rhythm they think would be appropriate to support and harmonize with the song being played.

- The person to the left of the second player listens to the two players, and then adds their complementary rhythm.

- The next person in turn listens to the song being created and plays their rhythmical contribution.

- This process continues until six participants in the circle are creating a playing ensemble.

- Then the starting player fades out of the ensemble.

- After the starting player stops, the seventh person layers in their rhythmical contribution.

- After the seventh player fully layers into the ensemble, the second player fades to silence.

- This processes continues until the moving ensemble goes all the way around the circle, reaches the starting player, and then includes them in the ensemble until it is again their turn to fade.
- When the starting player begins to fade this second time, the remaining players of the ensemble also fade to silence.

Participants engage fully in the process even when they are not actively playing: deep listening happens and when the final fade occurs everyone continues to listen to the deep silence.

A six person moving playing ensemble works well for a circle of fifteen to thirty participants. For a smaller circle of eight to ten recreational drummers, an ensemble of only three active players moving around the circle can be fun. With young children, and with beginning players, a five to six person moving playing ensemble helps maintain a solid groove. For large circles of fifty or so players, with two layers of seats, I create an evolving pie slice ensemble that moves around the circle.

Groove By the Numbers Games

Groove by the numbers games are based loosely on kids' rhythm games that I found in rhythmacultures in South Africa, Malaysia, India and Australia. Over the years I have seen many versions of these games being played by children and school teachers all over the world.

Kids in a Norway RAP

The foundation of these groove by the numbers games is that participants choose one or more numbers between one and eight. As the game facilitator counts from one to eight in continuous cycles, the players strike their instruments when their numbers are called.

These games help players learn how to place their foundational notes in a particular in-the-moment rhythm piece, solidifying their position in the melody line of the percussion song. Players learn to place their contribution into a group rhythm while they listen to the spaces between the notes being played. Once all the players are listening to each other, they can rely less on their numbers to decide when to play, and more on the rhythm song. The game facilitator can stop counting for the group once the song develops. Make sure that everyone in the circle agrees to let the melody line of the rhythm "settle down" before they contribute more notes in addition to their original choices.

These are facilitated games: the facilitator starts the rhythm verbally by counting cycles of one through eight and playing a note on the one and the five of each cycle. I like to play the first pulse on the lip of a cow bell to emphasize the one and then play the five on the top of the bell for a lighter sound – much like the ticking of a clock, "Donk dink Donk dink." For example:

The strikes	Donk				dink			
	I				I			
The count	(1)	2	3	4	(5)	6	7	8

Groove By the Numbers, Beginner Version

The beginner version of Groove by the Numbers teaches players how to place their notes as a contribution into a group rhythm, as they listen to the spaces between the other notes being played. These notes, once placed, offer a participant a foundation from which to express their rhythmical spirit in relation to other players.

Each player in the circle picks a number, between one and eight, that represents when they will play a note in the counted cycle. For example, if a player chooses the number three, this is their pattern:

```
     Strike                    Strike
     I                         I
1  2  (3) 4  5  6  7  8  1  2  (3) 4  5  6  7  8
```

Players also decide what type of sound to make with their instrument when they hit that note. Drummers choose between a tone, a slap, and a bass note. Hand percussion instrument players may choose a bell, shaker, or wood block, and their sound can be a ding, a shush or a doink.

Play the Game

- Participants choose their number.

- The game facilitator counts aloud from one to eight in cycles, while playing the one & the five on their bell.

- After the first cycle of counting, everyone in the drum circle plays on the number that they chose. As the count continues, players strike their instruments each time their number is called, and they continue playing that foundation note throughout the piece.

- The facilitator continues to count and play their bell on the one and the five until every player has joined the groove.

- Once the rhythm song solidifies, the facilitator stops counting aloud, de-emphasizing the numbers, so players focus on their musical relationship to the song.

- After a few more cycles, the facilitator stops marking the pulse with the bell.

- The facilitator invites players to improvise by embellishing their rhythm song with a few more notes.

- The facilitator joins the group, playing to complement and solidify the group's groove.

For beginners and younger kids, count slowly at first and then increase the tempo gradually as the groove solidifies.

I advise music and school teachers to run the gamut of possibilities with an all percussion circle first, then immediately afterward with an all drum circle, and finally with an ensemble of mixed instruments.

This game offers a great way to start an in-the-moment drum circle, leaving a lot of space in the music for interactive dialogue among the players.

Groove By the Numbers, Intermediate Version

The intermediate version of the Groove By the Numbers Game is played the same way as the basic game described above, except that every player in the circle picks two numbers between one and eight instead of one. While the basic Groove by the Numbers Game can be played by almost anyone who can count, the intermediate game is a little more challenging. Participants need to have basic playing skills and a sense of syncopation. The game helps participants learn to play two syncopated notes in a single rhythmical cycle.

Each player in the circle picks two numbers between one and eight, that represent when they will play notes in the counted cycle. For example, if a player choses the numbers three and five, this is their pattern:

```
    Strike Strike          Strike  Strike
      I      I                I       I
1  2  (3)  4  (5)  6  7  8  1  2  (3)  4  (5)  6  7  8
```

Play the Game

- Participants choose two numbers.
- The game facilitator counts aloud from one to eight in cycles, while playing the one & the five on their bell.
- After the first cycle of counting, everyone in the drum circle plays on the two numbers that they chose. As the count continues, players strike their instruments each time their numbers are called, and they continue playing those foundation notes throughout the piece.
- The facilitator continues to count and play their bell on the one and the five until every player has joined the groove.
- Once the rhythm song solidifies, the facilitator stops counting aloud. This de-emphasizes the numbers so players focus on their rhythmical relationship to the song. Facilitators need to be patient, as this settling process may take a few more cycles than when players chose a single number.
- After a few more cycles, the facilitator stops marking the pulse with the bell.
- The facilitator invites players to improvise by embellishing their rhythm song with a few more notes.
- The facilitator joins the group, playing to complement and solidify the group's groove.

This game invites more sophisticated interactions and can be rhythmically challenging. I sometimes play this intermediate version with recreational drum circles without starting with the basic game. However, in mixed groups such as community drum circles or beginning drummer circles I prefer to play the basic game first so players can build on their successes. Welcome to the magic of syncopation.

This game is a great groove starter for recreational drummers and drum circle enthusiasts.

Drum Strong

Outside Charlotte, North Carolina at the Misty Meadows Horse Farm, the first drumStrong Marathon has been organized to break the planet's record for the longest continuous rhythm drum circle ever held. We are drumming "crazy long to BEAT cancer" by raising awareness and funds for cancer education, survivorship support and research.

The 25 hour drum circle had started at midday the day before, and it is now 4:30 a.m. – a time in an all-night drum circle when deep drumming magic happens. Exciting party grooves happened late in the evening and now things have settled into trance grooves, "where there is nowhere to go 'cuz we're already there." The only challenge is that it is also Prom Night and quite a few teens are camping in the same meadow.

After partying all night, these young people are attracted to the drum circle and are joining us with their youthful exuberant party energy. They are not in tune with the circle's trance energy and are perhaps in a slightly altered state. The teens are disrupting the flow of the groove. Looking out on the disgruntled faces of the veteran drummers, I know I need to deal with the situation.

One commitment for this marathon circle is that the great mother bass drum will continue to play throughout the event. I bring the groove down

Welcome to Drum Strong.

to be very, very soft. While talking about the idea that the space between the notes is as important as the notes played, I initiate the Basic Groove by the Numbers Game. Everyone chooses a number and a sound and plays it as we find our way back to deep groove, including the post-prom-party drummers. Each player is "responsible" for one note only, initially, and takes ownership of the song. That groove lasts all the way past sunrise to morning, when more drummers join us for the final hours of the marathon.

Evolution Games

I designed evolution games to show how rhythms naturally change as part of any in-the-moment groove. These games accelerate the changes of rhythm patterns and melody lines in a non-scripted music-making environment. They are designed to be played with an ensemble of mixed percussion and drums. I offer several games in this book, and more evolution games in Volume Two.

Musical Chairs Evolution

The Musical Chairs Evolution Game is a simple orchestrational game that creates an opportunity to stand in the middle of a circle, make a personal choice and take action to experience the result of that choice.

Provide one less chair in the circle than the number of players. The person not seated becomes the chooser, who needs to find a place to sit down and play. They choose who will give up their seat and instrument and become the next chooser. For this evolution game the music evolves one instrument at a time.

This is a fun game for kids of all ages, and it works well in recreational drum circle environments.

Set up agreements with participants

1. A chooser cannot take back the instrument they have just given up.

2. A chooser can only pick people who have not yet been to the center of the circle.

3. Once the game progresses to the point that the person in the middle of the circle cannot remember who has not had a turn as chooser, they can yell "feet." As they play, those who have not yet been to the center of the circle raise one of their legs off the ground until the chooser picks someone to change places.

Play the Game

- The game begins with all the players sitting in a circle ready to play.

- The game facilitator does a call to groove to start a rhythm, and then becomes the first chooser.

- With the group in full groove, the chooser selects a person who is holding an instrument that they would like to play.

- The chooser walks up to the person playing the instrument, requests and receives that person's instrument and sits down in the vacated seat.

- The person who gives up their instrument and seat now goes to the middle of the circle to become the chooser.

- That person listens to the drum circle groove for a few rhythmical cycles before selecting the next person who will lose their seat and instrument.

- This is the short version of the game and is complete once everyone has a chance to be the chooser.

Create a longer version of the game by agreeing that any single instrument can be exchanged as many as three times during the game. This presents an opportunity for each player to become a chooser more than once, and any single instrument can be played by as many as four players during the game. This variation of the Musical Chairs Evolution Game encourages even more musical evolution.

Evolution From the Mixed Pile

The Evolution From the Mixed Pile Game uses an equal mix of drums and percussion with enough instruments for each player, plus a pile of instruments placed in the middle of the circle. I call these instruments the evolution pile. The group can self facilitate this game after the facilitator sets up the agreements for how to play and starts a groove.

As game facilitator, place a drum in every other seat, and a hand percussion instrument in the remaining seats before the event begins. Put extra drums in the middle of the circle and surround them with hand percussion. In addition to enough instruments for the players, you need a total of about a third again as many instruments for the evolution pile.

Set up agreements with participants

1. Each time a player goes to the center of the circle they either exchange their drum for hand percussion or their hand percussion for a drum. This agreement is important because most beginning players are drawn to drums over hand percussion.

2. Specify the order for players to make an instrument exchange.

   a. For a more controlled classroom situation, players take turns sequentially around the circle, one at a time.

   b. For a more mature group, the turns can be random and more than one person can make an exchange at the same time. After a player takes a turn, they need to wait until at least half of the other participants make an exchange before they take another turn. For a circle of twenty to thirty players, it works well to have no more than three players exchanging instruments at a time.

3. Encourage players to pay more attention to the ongoing changes in the rhythm than to the chaos that will be happening as people exchange their instruments at the evolution pile.

Play the Game

- Start a groove with every other player in the circle playing a drum and every other participant playing hand percussion.

- As the groove solidifies, participants take turns getting up to exchange their instrument with one from the evolution pile.

- Players go back to their seat and rejoin the ongoing, ever evolving groove.

Next, I describe a facilitated variation of the game called Evolution to Timbre.

Equal mix of drums and percussion

Evolution to Timbre Game

The Evolution to Timbre Game makes use of both a drum and a hand percussion instrument for every player. The facilitator sets up agreements for how to play, starts a group groove, and then facilitates the timbre evolutions. Players experience the different sounds when they evolve from playing a mixed variety of instruments to playing as an all-hand-percussion or an all-drum ensemble. The foundation for the Evolution to Timbre Game is the same for as Evolution from the Mixed Pile Game. Players will be facilitated to go between mixed, all drum, and all hand percussion ensembles.

As game facilitator, place a drum in every other seat, and a hand percussion instrument in the remaining seats before the event begins. Put enough extra drums in the middle of the circle for half of the players, plus one, and surround them with enough hand percussion for the other half of the participants. This setup includes enough drums for everybody to drum at the same time, and also enough hand percussion instruments for everybody to play them simultaneously.

Set up agreements with participants

1. Each time a participant goes to the center of the circle they either exchange their drum for hand percussion or their hand percussion for a drum.

2. This game is designed for a more mature group. The turns can be random and more than one person can make an exchange at the same time. After a player takes a turn, they need to wait until at least half of the other players make an exchange before they take another turn.

3. The facilitator calls out "evolve to all drums" to tell players it is time to switch to all drums or "evolve to all hand percussion" to tell them to move to all hand percussion.

4. The facilitator calls out "evolve" to tell players it is time to switch from either all drums or all hand percussion back to mixed instruments.

Play the Game

- Start a groove with every other participant in the circle playing a drum and every other player playing a hand percussion, just as for the Evolution from the Mixed Pile Game.

- As the groove gets going, all the people take turns getting up to exchange the instrument they are playing with one from the center of the circle. The number of players who get up at the same time depends on the facilitated agreements.

- Participants go back to their seat and continue to play in the ongoing groove.

- While the participants are playing, the game facilitator calls out "evolve to all drums."

- The players with drums stay in their seats and continue to play while the people with percussion get up and exchange from hand percussion to a drum from the evolution pile.

- Participants return to their seats and play their drums.

- Once everyone is in their seat playing a drum for a while the facilitator calls out "evolve," the agreed upon signal to start the evolution back to a mixed ensemble.

- All who were playing a drum before the "evolve to all drums" call will now take turns exchanging their drums for hand percussion.

- Once the circle is back to being a mixed instrument ensemble, the game continues with people taking turns exchanging the instrument they are playing with one from the center of the circle.

- While the participants are playing, the game facilitator continues the game by calling out "evolve to all percussion."

- The players with hand percussion stay in their seats and continue to play while the people with drums get up and exchange their drums for hand percussion from the evolution pile.

- Participants return to their seats and play their hand percussion.

(Game continued on next page)

- Once everyone is in their seat playing hand percussion for a while the facilitator calls out "evolve," the agreed upon signal to start the evolution back to a mixed ensemble.

- All who were playing hand percussion before the "evolve to all percussion" call will now take turns exchanging their hand percussion for drums.

- The circle returns to being a mixed instrument ensemble of drums and hand percussion, and the fun continues.

Players experience the evolution of the music as the timbres of the ensemble shift.

Evolution From the Tray

These three Evolution From the Tray games provide experiential training that focuses on the instrument composition of an orchestra. The game facilitator controls the evolutionary process in the circle.

These three games each have the same equipment setup: you need enough drums for everybody to drum at the same time, and also enough hand percussion instruments for everybody to play them simultaneously. The optimum combination of drums is an equal mix of low, medium and high pitched membrane drums. Ideally use one third bells, one third shakers, and one third wood instruments with variety in each timbral category to vary the sounds, pitches and tones.

Ensemble Evolution Game

The facilitator encourages players to listen to the changing timbres and pitches in the ensemble as they play the Ensemble Evolution Game. The drum circle evolves from all drums to all percussion and back.

Place a drum in front of each seat before the event begins. Keep the hand percussion instruments nearby to distribute during the game.

Play the Game

- Start with all the participants playing a groove on their drums.

- The game facilitator walks around the inside of the circle carrying either a tray or a large frame drum full of hand percussion. As they move around the circle, the facilitator chooses and gives an instrument to each drummer.

- Each player shifts from their drum to play their hand percussion when they receive an instrument. The music evolves, one instrument at a time, from all drums being played to all hand percussion playing.

- The facilitator enjoys the group groove with the players.

- Then the game facilitator goes around the circle with an empty tray collecting hand percussion instruments from the players.

- Each player shifts back to playing their drum when the facilitator collects their hand percussion. The music evolves, one instrument at a time, from all hand percussion back to all drums playing.

- After the drummers groove for a while, the facilitator can move around the circle, giving hand percussion to each drummer again, but starting with a different player in the circle. A new rhythm evolves.

Blind Date Orchestra Game

In the Blind Date Orchestra Game a facilitator does not know what they're going to hear musically until it unfolds. The circle evolves from an all hand percussion orchestra to a mixed ensemble as the facilitator shifts instruments among the players.

Before you start this game, be sure each player has a drum in front of them and a percussion instrument in hand.

Play the Game

- Start with all participants playing a groove on their hand percussion.

- The game facilitator walks around the inside of the circle with an empty tray retrieving a hand percussion instrument from every other person.

- Each player shifts to playing the drum in front of them when they give up their hand percussion. The music evolves, one instrument at a time, from all hand percussion to a mixed ensemble.

- Everyone listens to the groove for a while.

- Then the facilitator shifts the hand percussion instruments to the drummers by retrieving each instrument one at a time, and giving it to the drummer beside them in the circle.

- Each player shifts to play their new instrument as the facilitator goes around the circle. Those who were drumming now play hand percussion and the others start playing the drums in front of them. Each hand percussionist becomes a drummer and each drummer becomes a hand percussionist.

- The music evolves, one instrument at a time, with pitches and timbres evolving.

Selecting a Specific Orchestra

For the Selecting a Specific Orchestra Game, one person orchestrates at a time. They decide who in the drum circle will play which instrument. Participants learn how different combinations of instruments and players affect the quality of the ensemble and the the sound of their orchestra.

In this Evolution Game variation, the facilitator explains how to play the game and demonstrates by orchestrating the first round. Then the game facilitator turns the orchestration over to a volunteer in the circle.

Before you start this game, be sure each player has a drum in front of them and a percussion instrument in hand. Use an empty tray to collect hand percussion instruments.

Play the Game

- Start with all participants playing a groove on their hand percussion.

- During the groove, the orchestrator decides what types of drums they want to hear. They go around the circle, with an empty tray, collecting hand percussion instruments from participants who have the selected drums in front of them.

- The people who have been relieved of their hand percussion begin to play their drum.

- The orchestrator determines what mix of hand percussion they want to hear. They go around the circle again, with the tray of hand percussion instruments, exchanging percussion instruments with specific players.

- After everyone listens to a satisfying groove, the facilitator stops the groove and passes out hand percussion instruments to anyone who doesn't have one.

- Another volunteer takes a turn as orchestrator. They give hand percussion to specific drummers and retrieve hand percussion from other players so they can play the drum that is in front of them. The instrumentation of the orchestra evolves, creating new possibilities for creative expression.

Every different combination of instruments played by the ensemble creates an orchestra with a unique musical quality.

Groove Sharing Games

Groove Sharing Games empower individuals to set a foundational rhythm pattern that the other players in the circle will use as a platform to improvise and explore. When a beginner player shares their rhythmical spirit by modeling a pattern on the drum for the other players, the process begins to build their confidence. By learning someone else's rhythm pattern and then using it as a base for improvisation, the circle of players gain experience modeling new rhythms.

Share Your Groove

In the Share Your Groove Game, the groove originator sets the foundation for the whole circle by playing a simple pattern on their drum. Players model this basic rhythm and then add or subtract notes to develop a group groove.

This agreement game helps players develop their listening and improvisation skills. As they dynamically add or subtract notes, the players must listen to each other constantly and intently while they adjust their patterns to fit into the ever evolving drum circle song.

This is an all drum game that can be adapted to meet the needs of a mixed instrument ensemble. I advise music and school teachers who have enough time and equipment to run the gamut of options. Play these games first in a circle with all percussion instruments, then immediately afterward with an all drum circle, and finally play with an ensemble of mixed instruments. For recreational drum circles, facilitators can use this game to start a solid interactive groove for ten to more than a hundred players.

Sharing our groove in Scotland.

Play the Game

- The game begins with all the participants sitting in a circle ready to play.

- A volunteer groove originator establishes a foundational pattern from their seat, keeping their groove simple enough to leave room for the other players to improvise.

- Participants listen to the foundational groove for a few measures before they join in, playing the exact same pattern.

- Everyone in the circle plays that particular rhythm for several cycles to solidify the pattern.

- Then while the circle is in full groove, each player embellishes the rhythm to make their own pattern, adding or possibly dropping a note or two as they improvise from the original groove.

- Over time, the groove will settle into a solid interactive drum circle song.

In a structured school environment the game facilitator determines how long to wait before they bring the groove to a close. Then another player in the circle volunteers to be the groove originator. For a recreational drum circle, the music in the groove lets the players know when it is time to bring a song to a close.

Share Your Groove on the Run

Share Your Groove on the Run is an orchestrated game. While the drum circle is in full groove an orchestrator selects a player and gives them a continue-to-play signal. They then stop the other players to showcase the selected person, and invite the group to model and play the showcased rhythm, and then improvise from there.

This game gives each volunteer orchestrator an opportunity to go to the center of the circle and listen and then distinguish a rhythm that they think will provide a good foundation for improvisation. A player who wants to be showcased simplifies their pattern to create a basic rhythm. This raises that person's awareness about creating space between the notes in a pattern.

Play the Game

- While a drum circle is in full groove, a volunteer game orchestrator selects a player to showcase.

- The orchestrator gives a continue-to-play signal to the selected person.

- Then the orchestrator gives an attention call and a stop cut signal to all of the other players.

- The players stop.

- The remaining player showcases their rhythm by continuing to play.

- The game orchestrator invites the group to model and play the showcased rhythm.

- The group joins in, playing the modeled rhythm.

- Then the game orchestrator invites the players to improvise from the foundational pattern as they make up their own rhythms.

- A new groove is born, and the orchestrator returns to their seat.

- The group groove continues until the game facilitator selects another volunteer to take a turn as orchestrator.

A community drum circle facilitator can act as the orchestrator and use this game to change their group's groove on the run.

Share Your Groove on the Run, Agreement Version

You can turn the Share Your Groove on The Run game from an orchestrated game into an agreement game. This variation is a good game for drums only or for mixed percussion.

Play the Game

- The facilitator initiates the game by playing a pattern.
- The other players copy the pattern, to the best of their abilities, on their instruments.
- Once everyone is playing the same pattern, it becomes a platform for group improvisation and a new group groove is created.
- After 3 or 4 minutes of playing, the facilitator finds someone who is playing a pattern they think would make a good foundational rhythm for a different groove.
- With the group in full groove, the facilitator stops playing and gives a group attention call from their seat. When they have everyone's attention, they indicate (using a Disneyland point) who will be the next groove leader.
- The next groove leader continues to play their rhythm, while the rest of the players adjust their rhythm patterns (without stopping), copying the groove leader's pattern.
- When everyone is playing the same pattern, they can use it as another platform for group groove improvisation.
- After 3 or 4 minutes of playing, the groove leader selects the next foundational rhythm, gets everyone's attention and points to the next groove leader.
- You can repeat this process as long as you would like or until everyone has had a turn.

(This game does not appear in the DVD)

Drum Groove By Pitch Game

In the Drum Groove By Pitch Game, three volunteer groove originators each set a foundational rhythm for one of the three pitch groups in the circle. Members of each group then model the pattern played by their leader. After the three-part groove solidifies, everyone improvises. Players learn how the pitches of the three drum parts interact rhythmically to create a deeper, more integrated drum song.

The game facilitator first helps players identify whether they are playing a low, medium or high pitched drum.

1. Ask all the drummers to rumble together on the tonal area of their drum while listening to identify their drum's pitch.

2. Then, ask each pitch group to rumble separately to help players identify the members of their group who are scattered throughout the circle. If one drum pitch group has fewer members than the other two groups, the facilitator can shift a few players whose drum pitches are close to those of the smaller group. Then each group will have a similar volume when the group is in full groove.

Set up agreements with participants

1. Each player will model the pattern of the volunteer groove originator who is playing in their pitch range.

2. Players in the low pitched drum group will solidify their groove before the volunteer groove originator for middle pitched drums starts a complementary pattern.

3. The groove originator for the high drums will start their pattern after the rhythms of the low and middle pitch groups settle.

Play the Game

- After drummers identify their pitch groups, the game begins with all the players sitting in a circle ready to play.

- The game facilitator asks for one volunteer in each pitch group to be the groove originator.

- The person who is groove leader for the low drums plays a rhythm pattern.

- After listening for a few cycles, the players in the low drum pitch group copy the rhythm pattern of their groove leader.

- Then the groove originator for the medium pitch drum group listens to the low groove and plays a responding rhythm that complements the low groove.

- The players in the medium pitch group reproduce the pattern of their leader.

- The high pitch group groove originator listens to the low and medium drums, and then offers a related rhythm to complement their song.

- The drummers in the high pitch group copy the rhythm of their leader.

- Once all the drummers are playing a fully connected groove together, the game facilitator invites the players to use their rhythm patterns as platforms for musical improvisation.

Drum Circle Solo Games

D rum circle solo games create open space in the rhythm and showcasing opportunities for each individual player to "speak their spirit" on their instrument while being supported by the other players. These solos help Rhythmical Alchemy Playshop game participants grow rhythmical self-confidence and self-esteem.

Solos are sometimes scary for beginner players. When the group creates a safe non-judgmental space, each soloist then has a place to showcase their rhythmical expression using both their instrument and their voice in any way they want.

A drum circle in full groove connects everyone rhythmically. Then when the group stops their groove for a silent rhythm cycle, a soloist has space to speak their rhythm spirit on their instrument. While the soloist showcases their spirit, the group keeps time, and then comes back to the groove at the beginning of the next measure. This combination of groove and solo space encourages full creativity to emerge.

For most groups, such as family-friendly community drum circles and structured school environments, it is better to use these drum circle solo games after your group plays together long enough to be comfortable in full groove. An exception is that veteran recreational drummers may enjoy starting with solos at the outset of an event. Solos offer participants an opportunity to express themselves individually before moving on to more integrated listening games.

Groove to Solo Game

In the Groove to Solo Game, drummers play a groove for three measures and then come to a full stop for one measure. This creates space for a soloist to express themselves in the middle of a drum circle. I call whatever a drummer chooses to play, ranging from fancy rhythmically-challenging syncopated patterns to a single yelp of terror and anything between these extremes, a solo. This game is not a challenge to perform. It is an invitation, in the form of a four pulse space, for drummers to share their rhythmical spirits. Participants have an opportunity to learn how to express themselves during that space in an ongoing group groove.

Play the Game

- The game begins with all the participants sitting in a circle ready to play. They will take turns soloing in order, one at a time, around the circle. For beginning beginner players, the group facilitator may want to play a pulse on a bell or wood block during each solo space to support the soloist.

- The game facilitator gives a call to groove.

- The participants play a rhythm groove for three measures and then stop for one measure.

- In that single measure of silence, a player takes their turn to solo, even adding vocals for fun.

- At the end of the soloist's measure, the participants play the groove for three more cycles and then stop for the next player's one-measure solo.

If the game facilitator notices that players are having lots of fun and want to try new solos, they may decide to send the solo space around the circle more than once.

As facilitator, you can design your own unique solo game based on Groove to Solo. Be sure to set up any agreements about the parameters of your modified game with the players before you start. I offer some ideas for changes to the groove content, length of time between solos, and solo length.

- For middle schoolers and younger, everyone plays the same simple pattern as the ongoing groove.

- For community drum circles, high school students, and more mature groups, you can use an in-the-moment group groove.

- For veteran and advanced drummers, you can choose to use some culturally specific rhythms.

- Play the ongoing groove for one, two or three measures between each full stop for a solo.

- Plan for one or two measure solos for each soloist before the full group comes back in with the groove.

Groove
From Solo
to Duet

Elie Kihonia from the Congo and his friend Royal Taylor attend a community drum circle that I am facilitating at the Performing Arts Center near Pittsburgh, Pennsylvania. Elie and Royal are masterful drummers who are well known in the Pittsburgh drumming community. Each of them is playing respectfully relative to the other players, supporting the group groove with their rhythmical expertise rather than constantly soloing and showcasing themselves. Their occasional solos are short inspirational blasts of grace and beauty rather that long meandering diatribes full of flashy syncopated notes.

With such great drummers in the circle I know that sometime during the event I will showcase them to entertain and inspire the circle. When the time comes, I covertly facilitate my own variation of the Groove to Solo Game.

While we are in full groove I walk over to Elie and invite him to solo for one measure when I stop the circle. With his agreement, I return to the middle and count and signal the full group. While I make a stop cut, I also point to Elie and he fills the empty rhythm space with a graceful combination of notes. As he solos I silently count the other players back to groove so that when Elie finishes his one measure solo, the other players come back to full groove.

Three measures later I make another stop cut, again pointing to Elie and he plays another one measure solo. The stopped players now know what to do: they come back to full groove with minimal direction from me. The pattern is set and whether they know it or not, we are now playing the Groove to Solo Game.

While the group grooves for three more measures, I stand in the middle of the circle and nonverbally invite Elie's friend Royal to solo. As he nods yes I signal the group with an attention call and a stop cut, creating a solo space for him which he fills

with a beautiful combination of notes. At the end of another full groove cycle of three measures we create another silent solo space for Royal, which he again fills with masterful grace.

During the next group groove of three measures, I nonverbally invite Elie to solo for two measures. After he nods assent I hold up two fingers in the air to let the circle know we are going to stop for a two-measure solo break.

When the group stops, Elie plays a solo that is twice as long as his earlier one. We return to groove for three measures and then Royal takes a turn with a two-cycle solo.

Elie and Royal take turns soloing: first a full groove for three measures, then a solo by Elie for two measures, then three more measure of full groove followed by a solo for Royal. After a few of these solos, I signal for Elie to fill the first measure of the break and Royal to fill the second measure, which they do masterfully. Then we all return to the groove and more excitement as Elie and Royal share these two-measure solo dialogs three more times.

For the finale I signal both Elie and Royal to play a dialogue duet together during what would become the last two-cycle break.

As they dialogue together in the same two measure space, they bring the whole drum circle to a new level of excitement. Off we go into a different full groove that inspires a new level of rhythmical alchemy.

Call to Solo Game

Call to Solo offers each player in a drum circle an opportunity to decide to offer a solo when they are ready. While the group is in full groove, a player announces their commitment to solo by making an agreed upon call on their drum and with their voice. The other players answer the call with a prescribed unison response, and then stop to leave space for the one measure solo. The soloist then plays in that space, sharing their rhythmical spirit.

This game challenges players to announce their commitment to solo to the group and offers an opportunity for them to learn how to fit their solos between the full groove measures. Call to Solo is a simplified beginner's version of an advanced game I will describe in Volume Three of this Rhythmical Alchemy Playshop series.

Set up agreements with participants as you explain how to play the game. Players agree to:

- Play the same basic groove;

- Play a set call that will signal a desire to solo;

- Use a set pattern to respond to a call to solo, and then stop to create a solo space;

- Share the solo space, because more than one person can call to solo at the same time.

Play the Game

- The game facilitator starts the groove and everyone plays the same rhythm.

```
I    •    I    •    I    •    I    •
Gn        Gn   Go   Gn        Gn   Go
```

- The game facilitator sings and plays the call to solo pattern on their drum and invites players to echo the call. Everyone practices together by alternating between playing the groove pattern and then the call pattern a few times.

```
I    •    I    •    I    •    I    •
Pa        Pa   Pa   PaPaPa   Pa
```

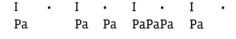

- The game facilitator teaches the pattern for responding to the call while the group is in full groove with the basic pattern. Then everyone practices the response together a few times, on the run.

```
I    •   I    •   I    •   I    •
Go  Go  Go  Go  GoDoGo  Go
```

- The facilitator then demonstrates the sequence. They play the call and the group answers and stops to provide a solo measure. The facilitator plays a solo measure and then the group and facilitator return to the groove pattern together.
- After demonstrating the call to solo a few times, as the group plays the basic groove the game facilitator asks for a volunteer to call for a solo and the game begins.
- If more than one person calls to solo at the same time, they all share the same solo space. When that happens, the players are encouraged to look at and listen to each other as they begin to play. The intention is to create an in-the-moment shared dialogue duet or medley.

As game facilitator you have lots of leeway to modify this game to match the age and rhythmical expertise of the group who will be playing. Ideas for variations of the game:
- For a younger group of kids, simplify the group groove.
- For beginners, simplify both the call and the group response patterns that players will use to signal a solo.
- In a recreational drum circle, invite the players to create their own in-the-moment groove instead of playing a set pattern in unison.
- For intermediate and advanced drum circle groups, lengthen the number of solo measures that the group creates for the soloist.

Be sure to set up any agreements about the parameters of your modified game with the players before you start.

Soundscape Experience

The morning after the Modern Music School's weekend Facilitators' Playshop in Germany, I stopped by the school's headquarters for a wrap-up meeting. I met with the music school company's president, his staff and a few of the music teachers who had participated in the program.

At the end of the meeting, Matais, one of the music teachers, commented that after he left the Playshop everything that he encountered had its own special rhythm and song. This ranged from a conversation among a group of women who he over-heard as he walked toward his car to the rhythmical gait of his own walk; from the song his shoes played as he stepped in the shallow rain puddles in the parking lot to the windshield wipers on his car as he drove home in the rain; from his wife's interactions with their kids as he entered their house to a water song that he heard for the first time when he took his evening shower.

When Matais woke up the next morning, he lay awake in his bed for a while before preparing for the day and the meeting that we were presently attending. He listened for the first time to the special rhythm and song that was "the symphony of his waking house" as his wife cooked breakfast and got the kids ready for school.

After almost tearfully describing to me his profound life soundscape experiences, his question was, "Is that the way it is for you after every Playshop you teach?" My honest and almost tearful answer to him was, "That is the way it is for me every moment of every day."

I am glad to have had the opportunity to guide Matais to experience what is my everyday rhythm bliss. That is the foundational mission in every Rhythmical Alchemy Playshop that I facilitate.

Closing

Playing these Rhythmical Alchemy Playshop games will give you the deep satisfaction of helping you and your friends uncover, discover and recover both the natural rhythmical spirits that you had as children and the magic of rhythm and soundscape experiences in your daily life.

Share your spirit and have fun.. Arthur Hull

extras

Learning Focus Summary

These Rhythmical Alchemy Playshop games embed several overall learning experiences:

- Creating a safe explorational environment where mistakes are not judged; instead they are considered as learning moments
- Cooperating in a dynamic environment that creates team building
- Listening for rhythmical and musical opportunities to improvise
- Improvising collaboratively
- Understanding the pitch and timbal makeup of a well-balanced percussion orchestra

Below are some of the specific learning focuses for each game described in the book.

Call to Groove Game – Everyone in the circle will learn to recognize the orchestrational signals, and how to respond to them. At the same time, players will learn how to use the signals themselves.

Rumble Wave Game – When the players in the circle respond to the signals, it builds confidence for the orchestrator and teaches the whole group about volume dynamics.

Rumble Point Game – This game teaches about pitches, drum circle song consciousness, and builds confidence.

Passing Games – These simple games are a great way to do team building with any age group. They naturally encourage peripheral vision and peripheral hearing in the participants.

Play What You Feel – This name introduction game is a fun and effective ice breaker for everybody that encourages self expression.

Basic Call and Response – This game encourages participants to express themselves within a specific time frame, and to explore rhythmical phrasing using one measure patterns.

Call and Response to Groove – This game teaches improvisation based on a set pattern that starts the groove.

Clap It to the Drum Game – This game educates the players in your circle about the importance of listening and dialogue and creating simple patterns to start a group groove.

Clave-Clap-to-Drum-Circle-Song Game – In this game the facilitator teaches a simple pattern that players use while they listen to the space between the notes and start a foundational groove. By altering their clapping patterns, players are able to listen to the overall rhythm without being distracted by drum pitches and timbres.

Air Drumming to Groove Game – This game teaches drum circle participants how to start a groove with simplified rhythm patterns that merge gracefully into a drum circle song.

Play My Name Game – This game introduces the concept of learning by listening and then singing a vocal rhythm before playing the pattern on the drum. Teachers can use it to set a foundation for singing rhythm patterns before playing them.

Sculpting a Song Game – This game offers participants opportunities to discover rhythmical interactions, dialogues and harmonies from the middle of a drum circle. Players then use their new awareness of these elements to improve their listening and interactive playing.

Layering in a Rhythm Game – This game emphasizes listening and collaborative rhythm making.

Layering Rhythm Dialogue Game – This game directs players' attention to the participants across the circle and encourages musical dialogue among them.

Layering in an Ensemble Game – This game helps players develop their awareness of the importance of individual contributions to a rhythm. Participants are encouraged to actively listen and appreciate the evolution of the music as the ensemble moves around the circle.

Groove By the Numbers Game – This game teaches players how to position their foundational note in a particular in-the-moment rhythm piece, solidifying their place in the melody line of the percussion song. This helps players learn how to place their contribution into a group rhythm, as they listen to the spaces between the notes being played.

Musical Chairs Evolution Game – This simple orchestrational game creates an opportunity to stand in the middle of a circle, make a personal choice and take action to experience the result of that choice.

Evolution From the Mixed Pile Game – This game accelerates the evolution of rhythm patterns and melody lines in a non-scripted music making environment and teaches players about these transformations.

Evolution to Timbre Game – This game uses the accelerated evolution process to teach players about the composition of all hand percussion, all drum, and mixed percussion ensembles.

Ensemble Evolution Game – This game encourages players to listen to the changing timbres and pitches in the ensemble as it shifts from all drums to all hand percussion and back.

Blind Date Orchestra Game – This game offers opportunities to listen to changes as the ensemble shifts from all hand percussion to a mixed circle, and from one mixed ensemble to a new one as timbres and pitches revolve around the ever evolving circle.

Selecting a Specific Orchestra Game – Participants learn how different combinations of instruments and players affect the quality of the ensemble and the sound of that percussion orchestra.

Share Your Groove Game – This game helps players develop their listening and improvisation skills.

Share Your Groove on the Run Game – This game teaches players to distinguish a rhythm they think will provide a good foundation for improvisation, and raises awareness about creating space between the notes in a rhythmical pattern.

Drum Groove By Pitch Game – Players learn how the pitches of three drum parts interact rhythmically to create a deeper, more integrated drum song.

Groove to Solo Game – In this game participants learn how to express themselves during a four pulse solo space that happens during an ongoing group groove.

Call to Solo Game – This game challenges players to announce their commitment to solo to the group and offers an opportunity for them to learn how to fit their solos between the full groove measures.

A family sharing rhythm spirit.

RAP Games and Music Education Standards

by Nellie Hill, MA Music Education

Each of these games can be used as a stepping-stone to addressing the National Standards for Music Education. Some achieve the standards on their own; some are the beginning part of a unit that works on a specific standard. This section will give ideas on how these can be used in your classroom. The national standards are as follows:

1. Singing alone and with others a varied repertoire of music
2. Performing on instruments, alone and with others, a varied repertoire of music
3. Improvising melodies, variations and accompaniments
4. Composing and arranging music within specified guidelines
5. Reading and notating music
6. Listening to, analyzing, and describing music
7. Evaluating music and music performance
8. Understanding relationships between music, the other arts, and disciplines outside the arts
9. Understanding music in relation to history and culture

When one first thinks of drum circle games, the assumption may be that the only standard covered would be #3 on improvising. The game sets that put an emphasis on helping students become comfortable creating their own patterns are Basic Call and Response, Call and Response to Groove, Layering in a Rhythm, and Layering Rhythm Dialogue Game. An extension to these games would be to divide the class into smaller groups and have each group use these techniques to perform a short composition that they create using these forms of dialogue. That activity touches on #2 (performing). We need to remember the repertoire should also include what our students create. They will also be composing music within specific guidelines! (#4).

Clap It to the Drum and Clave-Clap-to-Drum-Circle-Song Game are also perfect examples of composing and arranging music within specific guidelines (#4). Students must listen and dialogue with others. They learn about the importance of silences in music and how to best fit within the spaces of others. They are also beginning to listen to and analyze music (#6).

Groove By the Numbers Game is a great way to introduce students to both composing (#4) and notating music (#5). Once they have experienced the various levels of the game, you can show them grid notation, an easy step to notating parts. You draw a grid with 1-8 on the top and different instrument types down the side. Each instrument is assigned numbers in the grid and then the class plays the grid in a loop. You move from that to 2 sets of 8. Have the students create their own grid. And the best part… you can then show that the numbers are eighth notes, spaces are rests and they can write their grid in standard notation and they will truly understand the rhythmic relationships between parts!

The Share Your Groove on the Run is a wonderful way to use note reading and improvisation. In this game, students are to distinguish a rhythm that they feel would be a good foundation for improvisation. An extension of this game is after they have decided on the rhythm, they need to write it so that everyone can see it and the spaces it provides (#5 and #6). This would be a high level class but a great learning experience.

At all times during these games your students are evaluating music and music performance (#7), and are listening, analyzing and in the end describing what they have created (#6). The end result is that when they are given a traditional listening assignment they now have the skills to hear more of the parts, understand how they fit together and possibly why the composer made the choices. Their minds are more open to music that sounds "different," music of different cultures, etc.

By using these games in your classroom, your students will become critical listeners with an understanding of not only how to play music but how it is created. They will have been allowed to create music without the fear of being wrong. And you as a teacher will have accomplished two goals. You will have a curriculum that incorporates the Standards, and your music students will know that music is for everyone.

Book Recommendations

Drumagination, **with DVD, by Dave Holland.** A Rhythmic Play Book for Music Teachers, Music Therapists and Drum Circle Facilitators.

Interactive Rhythm, **with DVD, by Dave Holland.** Games, Songs & Interactions for the Music Educator, Music Therapist & Drum Circle Facilitator.

Rhythm Play!, **by Kenya S. Masala.** Rhythm Activities and Initiatives for Adults, Facilitators, Teachers, and Kids!

Rhythm Adventures, **by Tom Gill.** Exploring & Celebrating Creativity With Rhythm; A Hands-On Facilitator's Guide for Sharing Rhythm With Elders.

Rhythmic Kinesthetics, **with DVD, by Jeff Stewart.** Fun, Percussion-Based Activities & Games for the Classroom.

VILLAGE MUSIC CIRCLES™

Trainings and Playshops

Facilitating Human Potential Through Rhythm™

**You can lead any group
through a powerful rhythm experience**

Motivate · Inspire · Build Community

VMC: The Leader in DCF Trainings

- Providing successful leadership and DCF skills
- Based on Arthur Hull's facilitation techniques
- Over 35 years of Drum Circle Facilitation worldwide
- Drum Circle Facilitation Certification
- Continuing Education Credits

drumcircle.com

(831) 458-1946
Fax: (831) 459-7215
outreach@drumcircle.com

Weekend Facilitators' Playshop
Drum Call · Stop Cut · Sculpting
Prerequisite: None
Learn & practice facilitation skills, develop confidence, discover community.

Week-Long Intensive Facilitators' Playshop
Rhythmasizing · Orchestrating · Jump Time
Prerequisite: None
Learn & deepen facilitation techniques, develop professionalism, discover community.

Facilitators' Challenge Playshop + overlaps basic weekend Playshop
Integrating experience · Facilitating on the edge · Networking
Prerequisite: VMC returnee graduates only
Increase depth & breadth of technique through skills development and practice.

10-Day Advanced Mentor Leadership Training
Elders in Training · Mentoring · Leadership
Prerequisite: Completion of the Week-Long Intensive Playshop
A leadership training for community facilitators ready to mentor others through rhythm facilitation and community building processes.

About the Author

Often referred to as the father of the modern facilitated drum circle, Arthur Hull is a recognized pioneer and elder in what is now called the recreational music making movement. Since 1985 he has used Village Music Circles™ metaphors to build team spirit and promote unity in communities, schools, personal growth institutions and corporations worldwide.

A gifted rhythmatist and charismatic facilitator, Arthur leads diverse groups through joyful and inspiring experiences using music and rhythm. His wit and humor motivate people beyond their cultural and personal barriers and he inspires enthusiastic participation.

Since 1990 Arthur has provided professional trainings for community drum circle facilitators, music educators, school teachers and corporate trainers. He has trained over nine thousand facilitators in twenty-one countries.

Arthur also wrote the first drum circle facilitation handbook: *Drum Circle Spirit: Facilitating Human Potential Through Rhythm* in 1998. His second book *Drum Circle Facilitation: Building Community Through Rhythm* was published in 2006, and he authored an accompanying DVD with the same title.